Mimesis

Mimesis

The Literature of the Soviet Avant-Garde
Volume 2

Valery Podoroga

Translated by Evgeni V. Pavlov

VERSO
London • New York

This publication was effected under the auspices of the Mikhail Prokhorov Foundation TRANSCRIPT Programme to Support Translations of Russian Literature

 **transcript**

This English-language edition published by Verso 2024
Translation © Evgeni V. Pavlov 2024
Introduction © Ioulia Podoroga 2024
Originally published as part of *Mimesis: materialy po analiticheskoj antropologii literatury v dvuch tomach*
© kul'turnaya revolutsiya 2006, 2011
Every effort has been made to identify copyright holders for the images reproduced herein. The publisher will endeavour to rectify any omissions or inaccuracies once informed.

1 3 5 7 9 10 8 6 4 2

Verso
UK: 6 Meard Street, London W1F 0EG
US: 388 Atlantic Avenue, Brooklyn, NY 11217
versobooks.com

Verso is the imprint of New Left Books

ISBN-13: 978-1-80429-489-5
ISBN-13: 978-1-80429-490-1 (UK EBK)
ISBN-13: 978-1-80429-491-8 (US EBK)

British Library Cataloguing in Publication Data
A catalogue record for this book is available from the British Library

Library of Congress Cataloging-in-Publication Data

Names: Podoroga, V. A. (Valerii Aleksandrovich), author. | Pavlov, Evgeni
 V., 1975– translator.
Title: Mimesis : the literature of the Soviet avant-garde. Volume 2 /
 Valery Podoroga ; translated by Evgeni V. Pavlov.
Other titles: Mimesis. English
Description: London ; New York : Verso, 2024. | Includes bibliographical
 references.
Identifiers: LCCN 2024003601 (print) | LCCN 2024003602 (ebook) | ISBN
 9781804294895 (paperback) | ISBN 9781804294918 (ebk)
Subjects: LCSH: Mimesis in literature. | Russian literature – 19th
 century – History and criticism. | Avant-garde (Aesthetics) – Soviet
 Union. | Platonov, Andreï Platonovich, 1899–1951 – Criticism and
 interpretation. | Obèriu. | LCGFT: Literary criticism.
Classification: LCC PG3015.5.M56 P6413 2022 (print) | LCC PG3015.5.M56
 (ebook) | DDC 891.709/003 – dc23/eng/20240317
LC record available at https://lccn.loc.gov/2024003601
LC ebook record available at https://lccn.loc.gov/2024003602

Typeset in Minion Pro by MJ&N Gavan, Truro, Cornwall
Printed and bound by CPI Group (UK) Ltd, Croydon CR0 4YY

Contents

Introduction

The Analytical Anthropology of Literature

Ioulia Podoroga

This book is the second part of Valery Podoroga's monumental work on Russian and Soviet literature titled *Mimesis: The Analytical Anthropology of Literature*. The first book, published in English translation by Verso in April 2022, focused on the analysis of three prominent Russian writers from the nineteenth and early twentieth centuries. Additionally, it featured the preface from the original 2006 Russian edition, in which the author succinctly outlines the theoretical foundations underlying his approach to literature.[1] What follows is a brief overview of those foundations and the way they apply to authors like Gogol, Dostoevsky and Bely in the first volume of the book.

First of all, it is essential not to confuse 'mimesis' with its traditional meaning in classical literary criticism, as epitomised in the writings of Erich Auerbach and Paul Ricoeur, who themselves draw on Aristotle's ideas. In an effort to distance his approach from this tradition, Podoroga identifies three distinct types of mimesis that differ by the 'effect' of reality they intend to create. The first type, 'Mimesis-1', or external mimesis, aligns with the classical perspective to conceive literature as an imitation of reality, where the primary objective is to produce a strong 'referential

---

1 A few years after the first Russian edition the author revised his major work, dividing it into separate books, each dedicated to a single author (Gogol, 2018; Dostoevsky, 2019; Bely, 2020; Platonov/Shalamov, 2022; and the Oberiu, 2023).

illusion'. Storytelling and narration are based on this mimetic relationship. 'Mimesis-2', internal mimesis, is a procedure employed by a writer *within* his or her work. It involves a keen focus on the mimetic forces of language operating inside the (literary) work, helping to construct and consolidate its wholly self-sufficient and self-contained world. Instead of aiming to reproduce a plausible 'real-world' situation, it interacts with the external world in a peculiar manner. Often, it directs its own unique vision of the world against the 'real' world. The third type, 'Mimesis-3', emerges from communication and exchange among various literary works, including mimetic connections, mutual confrontations, borrowings, or conscious or unconscious influences. Each form of writing can be viewed as a combination of these three types of mimesis, but it is the inclination toward internal mimesis (Mimesis-2) that distinguishes the literary tradition that holds a special fascination for Podoroga.

Throughout his analysis of literature, Podoroga deals with authors who practise this type of mimesis and exemplify what he categorises as 'other' or experimental literature.[2] 'Other' literature adopts a stance contrary to that of the Russian realist (imperial) canon, which Podoroga also refers to as 'courtly-noble', 'classicist' or 'example' literature. In contrast to the traditional realist novels by authors like Tolstoy, Turgenev, Chekhov, etc., the 'other' literature embraces a different image of reality, which is based paradoxically not on the imitation of the other, but on the imitation of oneself, as long as the author's 'I' deeply penetrates and modifies sensible and sensual layers of reality. The purpose of Podoroga's research is to describe the emergence of a literary work through this internal mimetic process that avoids external objectivation.

While some scholars argue that Russian literature lacks a defined notion of form when compared to Western literature, Podoroga embarks on exploring this kind of form – an organising principle that governs each literary work. Each author is driven by a 'will-to-work' that cannot be verbalised. In the course of diligent analysis, one can discern where and how this will-to-work manifests itself, identifying its signs and effects, which ultimately give rise to a new form. Embracing the role of an attentive observer, Podoroga invites us to approach the writer's work as if exploring an entirely unfamiliar and alien world, necessitating decryption. Why so? Because of a fundamental time rift: engaging with texts from

---

2   Podoroga is not exclusively interested in Russian literature; among his favorite authors are Kafka, to whom he devoted his last book, as well as Proust and Beckett.

a different epoch – being unable to restore the time to which they originally belonged – requires adopting an 'anthropological approach'. As an 'anthropologist of literature', one must refrain from premature judgements based on preconceptions and interpretations. Instead, the text should be treated as an array of unfamiliar documents and 'facts', disentangled from any pre-existing theories. In this vein, Podoroga emphasises the primacy of construction over interpretation as he formulates his analytical credo: 'construction first!' The anthropological approach guarantees objectivity, insofar as it provides the means of 'direct cognition' of the underlying constructive principles within a literary work.

Each of the three parts of the first volume of *Mimesis* is preceded by an introduction that serves as an original entry into the literary work of the studied author. The introduction to Gogol revolves around the artistic genre of the still-life, conveying a peculiar state of things – between life and death. The visual representation of still-life mirrors the entropic temporality of Gogol's novels and foreshadows the central concept of 'the heap', crucial for Podoroga's analysis of Gogol's work. Moving to the study on Dostoevsky, the introduction sets the stage for further investigation, exploring the theme of violence that profoundly influences Dostoevsky's writing. The picture *The Body of the Dead Christ in the Tomb*, painted by Hans Holbein the Younger, provides an archetype for Dostoevsky's obsession with cruelty and various forms of bodily suffering. It is complemented by an image of a tarantula from Hippolyte's dream (in *The Idiot*), provoking a reaction of horror and repulsion that will be associated with evil and malicious characters in Dostoevsky's novels ('red bugs'). As to Andrei Bely, Podoroga's introduction delves into the idea of 'making-strange' (estrangement or defamiliarisation), an analytic strategy elaborated by Russian formalists, as a guiding principle. Bely's rejection of reality, as a result of this strategy, represents a complete reversal of the traditional concept of mimesis.

In the first part of the book, 'Nature Morte: The Order of Work and Nikolai Gogol's Literature', Podoroga singles out three major categories of Gogol's poetics: laughter as a unique way to access Gogol's world; the image of the heap and of its rhythmic number as the main feature of Gogol's thinking and imagination; and the role of language as a way of exploding the grammatical and lexical conventions of the dominant 'imperial' Russian language. All these elements intertwine and enrich each other as Podoroga's analysis progresses.

Reading Gogol means laughing, but this laughter is not generated by an object. We do not laugh *at* something, but the power of laughter supersedes everything, even overcoming language itself, thus calling into question the sense of reality. It is a universal laughter mingled with fright, insofar as its mimetic force destabilises the world, creates chaos. Podoroga argues that Gogol's technique of mimesis operates through one single image that includes all its possible modifications: the world, in its every manifestation, is viewed as a heap. This image both corresponds to the ancient Greek idea of Cosmos and can also serve as a Russian equivalent for the romantic notion of Chaos. In Gogol's poetic ontology, it represents a universal symbol of the whole. When reading Gogol, we can easily make a list of heap-like images: all forms of rubbish, junk, lumps, collections of objects, items of clothing, assortments of food, etc. Podoroga claims to have found as a constructive marker of the heap a minimum rhythmic count of heaps: 7 (+/-2). This number regulates what is assembled, how it comes together and how it disintegrates. It displays a rhythm of the construction of the image of the heap and its projection onto the sensual material of experience. The heaps can be of three kinds: numerable, innumerable, and being (currently) enumerated. The rhythmic harmonious whole is the literary work itself. Enumeration, whether of animate or inanimate creatures, never encloses and completes Gogol's world. There is always a touch of chaos that risks putting everything at stake. Everything in this world tends to fall apart and is subject to depletion. The innumerable is chaotic, devoid of form, counting homogeneous entities and things as if they were part of primordial matter.

Gogol was a great collector of 'little words' coming from different regions of the Russian Empire, above all the little-Russian (Ukrainian) lexicon. Podoroga shows how these words destabilise the language by introducing elements of chaotic disorganisation. Devoid of any determinate meaning, they can be easily bestowed with whatever significance the reader would like them to carry. In this sense, they possess an explosive power, resisting the imperial dominance of the literary comprehensive tradition. These words serve as both material for laughter (due to their strange, even absurd form) and ideal elements for creating a 'language-heap'. Gogol's anti-literariness and agrammatism, emphasised by many scholars, are not disadvantages, but assets that lead to the invention of a new language. Its marginal status allows it to successfully counterweigh the standards adopted by the Russian language used in the great imperial canon of literature.

One of the main features of the 'other', experimental literature is its relationship to time. In Gogol's works, time takes on the quality of animating the dead and deadening the living, akin to a still-life painting. The characters come to life for a very brief moment and then freeze again. They appear and disappear almost by accident, as if reality itself occurs by chance. Time in Gogol's world is composed of such small incidents, random appearances that are fleeting and instantaneous. This renders a conventional narrative with motives, causal development, and so on, impossible. The culmination of this singular temporality is evident in the final 'apocalyptic' scene, such as the one in *Inspector General*, where the news strikes and forever immobilises the characters.

The second part of the book, 'The Birth of the Double: The Logic of Psychomimesis and Fyodor Dostoevsky's Literature', is the most ambitious section, given the extraordinary range of analytical tools used and the intricacy of the problems it deals with. Firstly, Dostoevsky's 'workbooks' reveal how unusually he worked with the manuscripts of his novels: rather than successful planning, the process is characterised by failure and 'anti-planning'. The planned elements constantly react to sudden changes, causing the plan itself to shift (sometimes radically), as if the author-narrator is unable to keep up with it. All events, even those predicted, occur suddenly, so that the plan fluctuates, loses its stable contours, gets remodelled and refined. Planning becomes a goal in itself, and each novel is just one of the multiple possible scenarios projected by Dostoevsky. Dostoevsky's planning encompasses four areas that extend beyond literature. These are: the epileptic plan, which designates the suddenness of a cerebral attack and draws a pattern of seizures; the dream plan, coinciding with the sudden rapidity of shifting images that reveals the true meaning of the real; the debtor's plan, associated with the threat of punishment, which provokes acceleration in writing; and the game plan, linked to the expectation of a sudden lucky (or unlucky) number falling out. Finally, there is the plan of plans, which has its counterpart in the apocalyptic plan, encompassing all other plans and constituting the literary work as such with its unique experience of time. In each of these plans, the same operative form of temporality dominates: 'suddenly-time'. 'Suddenly' moments provoke an instantaneous acceleration of time. This is why the spatial images in Dostoevsky's novels are so unstable and hard to examine. Among his favourite techniques is compression. Compressed time is unable to fit into a linear 'realistic' chronology. It does not refer to the remote future or past, it hardly covers 'yesterday' and 'tomorrow', and it always tends toward an end; what matters is what is about to happen – sudden change, catastrophe, scandal. It is rich with the effects of surprise, indicating the unpreparedness of the protagonist's (or the narrator's/ author's) personality for the upcoming change. In 'suddenly-time', there is no evolution, no order in time, but everything occurs simultaneously.

Podoroga describes Dostoevsky's 'threshold' sensibility by investing this word, borrowed from Bakhtin, with a psychomimetic meaning. If Dostoevsky's heroes 'feel' excessively, if they are open and vulnerable to the world, it is because they lack corporeal, spatial boundaries. Their bodies cannot be related to those of others. Unlike the realist tradition, Dostoevsky's heroes cannot be localised and described as inhabiting a given environment, communicating with other people, moving in a determined space or direction. They do not have proper biographies and even their death has no particular meaning, as death itself is not problematised. The touch is prohibited in the sense that physical contact, decisive for realistic literature, is absent from his novels. The perspective or depth required for a realistic depiction of characters is not the concern of Dostoevsky. Instead, his characters are embodied through a threshold sensibility, trespassing the boundaries and borders: they are affectively involved in a conflict of forces, vibrating as in convulsions, spasms, hallucinations or (day-)dreams, torn between contradictory impulses that they fail to reconcile.

The last chapter of this second part, 'The Ideal Chronicler', is devoted to the structure of narration, providing Podoroga with an opportunity to conduct a sharp criticism of Bakhtin's seminal book on Dostoevsky. He calls into question the use of concepts such as voice, consciousness, hearing and meaning. Bakhtin understands the voice as communication between two voices at least: mine and that of the other. This voice is equal to the consciousness and always embedded in meaning. But most of the voices in Dostoevsky's novels do not express or announce something; instead, they constitute a kind of 'sonorous primary matter', creating interferences more than complete statements. Hearing is different from listening. The reality of Dostoevsky's novels is presented through a play of noises, sounds, yelling or murmuring that cannot easily be referenced or spatially localised – one needs to listen carefully in order to distinguish what is being said. Curiously enough, argues Podoroga, Bakhtin neglects Dostoevsky's own theory of consciousness and substitutes it with his own idea of dialogue. Yet, the absence of independent consciousnesses makes the idea of dialogue void. Characters, rather than engaging in a dialogue as traditionally understood, cross each other's paths and let themselves be carried away in the orbit of the character they have just encountered.

The third and final part of the book, titled 'Literature as Self-consciousness: The Experience of Andrei Bely', offers a three-staged approach to Bely's literature. Firstly, it investigates the central idea or image of explosion, intrinsic to Bely's world. Secondly, it addresses the theory of time that Podoroga refers to as 'blink-of-an-eye' time. And finally, it unfolds a psychoanalytic mechanism of 'scissors', which originates in Bely's relationship to his parents and compulsively repeats itself throughout his artistic biography and self-reflections.

A writer, poet and one of the prominent theoreticians of symbolism, Bely, however, is less known and read abroad. Podoroga's interest emerges in relation to Bely's modernist type of writing that belongs entirely to the experimental literary movements of the early twentieth century. Reality enters Bely's literature through the mimesis of the explosion. Thematically, the explosion is at the centre of the novel *Petersburg*, but, as Podoroga argues, everything in Bely's poetic universe becomes potentially explosive. One must distinguish the explosion as a mimetic form, in charge of the relationship between the characters in the narrative, from the explosion underlying the construction of a literary work: the 'poetic cosmology' it initiates. The explosion on a cosmological level reduces everything to nothing, forms to formlessness. But it also produces 'swarms' and 'holes', which correspond to different stages of the explosion. The (black) holes correspond to the scarcity and porosity of the world but are nonetheless full of energy that accumulates and leads to an explosion. The hole is nothingness, but it is also refuge (*regressum ad uterum*) and in this sense tends to be filled. The swarms, on the contrary, signify the surplus of matter that scatters everywhere after an explosion takes place. This pair duplicates itself on several levels of representation that can be identified in Bely's writings: emptiness versus fullness, form versus contents, space versus time.

The pressure of explosive problematics on Bely's imagery system is especially intensified after the Revolution of 1905 (earlier, it was more of an aesthetic experience anchored in the apocalyptic tradition of Russian thought). The explosion is indeed a physical phenomenon (all sorts of catastrophes, natural or not), but it is also a figure of temporality. Time explosively attacks unconsciousness, while consciousness is excluded from the experience of temporality. Bely's experience of time sheds light on his philosophy of the mimetic. The moment, as a particle of time, is a generation of the explosive character of temporality. Bely's time is equal to a blink, very fast. 'Suddenly-time' is of course unpredictable, but Dostoevsky's narrator does all he can to anticipate those moments. A 'blink-of-an-eye' cannot be grasped at the moment of its passing but only through the traces it leaves in memory. Podoroga precisely analyses different aspects of the blink-of-an-eye time: physical (blinking), temporal (instant), mnemic (flashbacks), ontological (time as an indivisible unit).

The symbol of the scissors, conceptualised by Podoroga in relation to Bely, indicates the painful conflict between father and mother, with Bely as a child being torn apart between them; it becomes then the sign of a dead-end, of the insolvability or hopelessness of any decision or any move in life. But, according to Podoroga, Bely manages to transform it positively, resulting in the strategy of a making-strange of everything, including oneself. Bely rejects the unity of the 'I'; this 'I' has already estranged itself.

The present volume, divided into two parts, examines the works of notable figures of the Soviet avant-garde movement: Andrei Platonov, on one side, and the Oberiu (Union of Real Art) group, which included Daniil Kharms, Leonid Lipavsky, Aleksander Vvedensky, Yakov Druskin and Konstantin Vaginov, on the other. Guided by the mimetic approach he employs as his main analytical tool, Podoroga reveals the structure of Platonov's utopian narratives through the image of 'the Machine'. Platonov's characters imitate machines, seeking to merge themselves with the mechanical. The mechanistic perspective operates as inherently objective, devoid of any emotional involvement. Simultaneously, these narratives depict vast expanses of empty spaces, peculiar wastelands that are inhabited by characters – wanderers and warriors alike – who, in contrast, yearn to immerse themselves in Nature. This tension between Nature and the Machine, as Podoroga demonstrates, forms the core of Platonov's literary outlook. The figure of 'the Eunuch of the soul', which Podoroga brings to the fore in his analysis, occupies the place of the observer: only he (another 'I'), to whom the soul is absent, can behold these desolate, post-revolutionary spaces with the appropriate distance. Being part of the non-human process of 'emptying out', this observer becomes capable of transcending all limitations and viewing Death as a new beginning.

What the 'Machine' is to Platonov's mimetic strategy, 'Chance' is to the Oberiu poetics. Their poetic ontology can be defined in terms of chance (understood as a random occurrence or incident) as a way of relating to time and overcoming reason and its logic. The chance marks the moment when time comes to a halt. What is happening does not belong to the chronological time punctuated by subsequent events: it is solely generated within the realm of language. This results in a division between language and the world (reality), which creates an absurdist effect. Each of these writers addresses the problem of chance differently. Kharms delivers a performative scenario of chance as an unmotivated incident. Druskin, the in-house philosopher of the group, theorises the concept of a 'small deviation', which also captures the attention of Lipavsky, Vvedensky and Kharms. All attempts to examine 'chance' are directed against the 'world-time' and introduce diverse temporal experiences or experimentations with time: cataleptic or frozen time, time perceived by no one as it lacks a subject, the cessation of time, and more. Each of these requires a poetic portrayal, which the Oberiu poets strive to attain.

The concepts, or rather unifying images, that Podoroga works with pertain to the mimetic attitude elaborated by each author. They represent a driving force that counters the traditional idea of mimesis, as they do not mimic a certain 'objective' idea. It is not a mimesis of imitation but that of production, where the order of temporality plays a key role. In his approach to literature, Podoroga mobilises various theoretical strategies and critical commentaries from literature studies, but his foremost inspiration is philosophical: how does literature produce an independent way of thinking, distinct from that of philosophy but capable of taking into account the primordial acts of thinking that philosophy is not usually interested in. What, then, is the reality of the (literary) work and how can one (the anthropologist of literature) get access to it? The significance of Podoroga's perspective on the relationship between literature and philosophy arises from his awareness of the original and unique experience that literature can offer to philosophy. Rooted in the phenomenological analysis of human sensibility, its 'being in the world', his philosophy remains highly receptive to a variety of experiential forms, particularly the kind cultivated by literature. Mimesis and Time are two primary factors that Podoroga identifies as shaping the singularity of the literary experience.

Pavel Filonov, *The Tractor Workshop at the Putylovsk Factory* (1931)

PART I

Eunuch of the Soul: 'Revolutionary Machines' and the Literature of Andrei Platonov

Introduction

Homo ex machina: On the Contemporary State of Machinism

A motif of a poor machine, on a river's bank, in a stillness of nature.[1]

Kharms' room was 'more or less ascetically furnished',
but there was a metallic strikingly large something:
  - What is this?! - an amazed visitor would ask.
  - A machine.
  - What kind of machine?
  - Not any particular kind. Just a machine.
  - Ah . . . and where did you get it from?
  - I put it together myself! Kharms would answer not without pride.
  - And what does it do?
  - It doesn't do anything.
  - What do you mean doesn't do anything?
  - Just like that, it does nothing.
  - Then why do you need it?
  - I simply wanted to have a machine in the room.[2]

---

1   Andrei Platonov, *Zapisnye knizhki* [Notebooks], Moscow, 2000, 73.

2   Vladimir Lifschitz, 'Mozhet byt' prigoditsya' [It might be useful], *Voprosy literatury* [Problems of literature] 1 (1969), 241.

The Avant-Garde and Its Machines:
The Aesthetics of New Form

At the centre of the European and Russian avant-garde there is the Great Machine in its various hypostases. Unlike the epoch of modernism that did not yet have a real interest in science, its technical capabilities and its machines, the avant-garde adopted the machine as a kind of new, higher Reality that replaced the old one – the reality of Nature. The machine that pushes out the natural is the coming, 'human-less' new Nature. After all, what is Revolution, if not the process of creating a new reality with the help of a fantastic megamachine?

At times we get a strong impression that there is no such clear and definite distinction between modernism and the avant-garde when it comes to the Machine.[3] The machine is either accepted or rejected: if it is accepted, all mimetic functions are transferred unto it, it is imitated, as if it were a necessary condition of total mimesis. If it is rejected, then it is only in favour of the human capacity for imitation: to imitate means to recreate in the machine something human, to humanise it. Hence the late avant-garde's play with the machine as the subject of individual ethics. The surrealists tried to end the superiority of the machine by placing it as a negative object at the centre of their strategies. Countless impossible machines emerged, 'machines that don't work' and that produce nothing. The fear of the machine weakened when the machine became human. It is not the machine that pushes out the human being in order to take his or her place, it is the human being who wants to become a machine. The machine that is detached from a human being, that has acquired an independent individual existence – this is the old impossible myth. The conclusion: we've been inside a machine for a while now. The machine has a much better imitational power than the human body. Now it carries out a complete mimesis of reality, giving us the real in a machinic form (or, today, in a digital form).

One of the avant-garde's most important achievements is the de-anthropologisation of the world, meaning the mechanisation of sensibility

---

3   In the modernism of Kandinsky and Klee, or the avant-garde of Malevich and Filonov, we find grand theories of art, collections of methods and techniques that the artist must follow to realise the will to a new form. All of them share a common will for the (creative) Work. They support the old cult of the Master-artist, who 'manually' bypasses all mediation of machines and technical devices, who creates a new world from nothing. The figure of the Master weakens the differences between this modernism and

and all the possibilities of perception. The effect of alienation is the most general characteristic of the aesthetic. What does it mean to be a machine? Is it a misfortune or a joy?

> All the people you see, all the people you know, all the people you may get to know, are machines, actual machines working solely under the power of external influences, as you yourself said. Machines they are born and machines they die . . . But there is a possibility of ceasing to be a machine. It is of this we must think and not about the different kinds of machines that exist. Of course, there are different machines; a motorcar is a machine, a gramophone is a machine, and a gun is a machine. But what of it? It is the same thing – they are all machines.[4]

The machine is not what is controlled, but a part of the environment, it is society's material unconscious, in which is developed the form of the human being that became machinic. This is the total machinic Mimesis: the reworking of the human in favour of the new master of being – the Machine. It is precisely the machine that does not simply establish the connection with the outside world; it is not just a model of cognition, but being itself. To think, to want, to suffer, to work is to be a machine.[5]

In a number of articles, Rosalind Krauss attempts to demonstrate that modernism or the avant-garde, or that which in artistic experience seeks to speak on behalf of the new, original and genuine – these essential characteristics of the work of art – rests on the spirit and the matter of the primordial: the *grid* ('the construction of the World').[6] The originality and novelty of an artistic gesture is limited by the extent to which it is able to turn to deep layers of sensuous experience. However, if we follow the

---

the avant-garde. (See also Dmitri Sarabyanov, 'K ogranicheniyu poniatiya avangarda' [Toward limiting the concept of avant-garde], in *Russkaya zhivopis'. Probuzhdenie pamiati* [Russian painting: The awakening of the memory], Moscow, 264–75.)

4 · P. D. Ouspensky, *In Search of the Miraculous: Fragments of an Unknown Teaching*, London: Routledge and Kegan Paul, 1977, 19.

5 See Jonathan Flatley, 'Art Machine', in Nicholas Baume ed., *Sol LeWitt: Incomplete Open Cubes*, The Wadsworth Athaneum, MIT Press, 2001, 83–101.

6 Rosalind E. Krauss, *The Originality of the Avant-Garde and Other Modernist Myths*, Cambridge, MA: MIT Press, 1985 (see the chapters 'Grids', 'The Originality of the Avant-Garde' and 'LeWitt in Progress'). See also Rosalind E. Krauss, *The Optical Unconscious*, Cambridge, MA: The MIT Press, 1973, 1–30.

principle of the grid, we can erase everything that is found on the surface of the world which would make it difficult to discern the foundational grid. There is no blank surface that has not been previously gridded and divided into cells. A creative act is a projection on the surface of a *tabula rasa* ('blank slate') of an event that never happened. Is it possible to recognise that the avant-garde has some special spontaneity that creates a world, a spontaneity that would not be reducible to modernism (that would not be modernist)? For, in our definition, the avant-garde consciousness – or, more broadly, leftist art as such (Brecht, Vertov, Platonov, Filonov or Khlebnikov) – is a revolutionary consciousness. Where it takes place, it opens up an aspect of the world defined by the explosive nature of changes. The avant-garde consciousness balances between destruction and renewal (a 'new beginning'.) This beginning is the very goal of the destruction. The destruction indicates the possibility of beginning again, and the more radical the destruction, the more devastating the novelty. 'Show me how well you can destroy, and I will tell you what sort of avant-gardist you are!'

Thus, the avant-garde gesture is the gesture of complete negation (i.e. the sort of gesture that is devoid of any features of affirmation). A decisive 'no' is juxtaposed with an infinite set of partial affirmations of 'yes'. This decisive 'no' contains a cessation of all possible temporalities of everyday life. Krauss' ironic-critical message is that the avant-garde is credited with the positive task of 'representing' authenticity, originality and novelty. In reality, the avant-garde creates copies, or becomes a general neutral foundation for creating copies of everything. The avant-garde is an ideal copier-machine. And all this is due to the fact that, while evaluating an avant-garde artist in terms of novelty, progressivity and innovation, we count as avant-gardists a lot of very different artists; as a result, we confuse the avant-garde with the avant-garde consciousness. Is it permissible to allow for such confusion to exist? In reality, the avant-garde and avant-garde consciousness are much later phenomena in the artistic experience of the world. And not only later, but also short-lived (and remarkably unstable, even if rich in consequences). Not every artist is an avant-gardist, but only those who choose to question all previous art. The grid has long served as an important bridge between reality and its reflection; it was the 'most authentic' copy. If the avant-garde artist negates classical art, then it is only because of the latter's uniqueness and originality, while he himself creates something repeatable, something that constitutes itself as a copy of everything.[7] His ability to create models, clichés, programmes, stereotypes and so on, means that reality must be eliminated through algorithms of repetition.

Even if we highlight the decisive characteristics of the avant-garde or the modernist consciousness, they cannot help us organise a field of relations in the powerful wave of artistic practices of the beginning and the middle of the twentieth century. The avant-garde work of art is the collectivist distribution of Truth (unified global form). The avant-garde artist perceives himself to be the messenger of an invisible collective (that consists of those like him), and therefore attempts to de-individualise his manner of creating things. The Machine is of great help here. If we look at the classical figures of modernism (Klee, Kandinsky, Mallarmé, Proust or Joyce), we will see that everywhere the emphasis is on creating a special theoretical model of Mimesis, which is primarily a personal achievement of the Master. In modernism we find the last attempt to restore the general picture of the world, what Klee called 'a site of cosmogenesis', but to do so exclusively on the basis of individual positions. The individual expression of experience is clearly not related to the avant-garde project. The Master declares his authorship of a particular Cosmos that he recreated. The subject matter of his concern is the language which he must use to address his viewer. He develops a special artistic language, a dictionary-collection of elements, on the basis of which a work of art can be constructed. The world is represented in its individual properties that are not reducible to collectivist properties. This, in my opinion, is the radical difference between the owner-individualist, the artist-thinker

---

7   But here's what's interesting: the avant-garde in this sense is a purely extensive production of images, as opposed to modernism which tends to overestimate the intensity, and thus to put forward the symbolic interpretation. The distinction between two interpretations of the work of art in the art of the avant-garde is interpreted by Krauss very broadly: one is based on its centrifugal dynamics, the other on its centripetal dynamics. In the former case, the work of art is pushed beyond its own limits, it is a fragment of a grandiose picture of the world from which it does not separate itself; in the latter case, on the contrary, the work of art is a place in space-time into which collapses an entire world; it is Leibniz's monad, which reflects the whole world in a drop of water: 'The grid is an introjection of the boundaries of the world into the interior of the work' (Krauss, *The Originality of the Avant-Garde*, 19). This difference, in my view, can be translated into a plane of relationship between the extensive and the intensive, which would separate the avant-garde consciousness from the modernist one. Krauss herself, however, insists that this distinction (between interpretations) is relative, and its acuity disappears when it comes to specific works of art. (Ibid., 19–21.)

Kandinsky and the commissar of arts and the 'universal artist' Malevich. (Of course, this does not contradict the fact that in artistic practice their creative manners can influence each other.) In the Russian avant-garde, the figure of the Master was the outpost of collectivist self-consciousness.

Machine, *modus operandi*

A machinist. Every machine has a secret, and this secret is a machinist. After all, all the most important ontological characteristics of machinism cannot be applied without some carrier of free will ('open conscious-ness'). For example, machinic consciousness in Platonov splits into three hypostases: the Master (he who does something), the Machinist (he who controls it), and the Observer (he who observes it – 'eunuch of the soul'). Platonov's main hero is always the Master (with a capital letter), the one who creates something with his own hands (and not necessarily only a technically complex something); here we see the obvious superiority of manual labour. Machines, such as a steam locomotive, a motorcycle, a dynamo-machine, a turbine and so on, were made by someone, but not always by the one who admires them and puts them in motion (some-times Platonov's heroes believe that machines have created themselves). Such machines are admired, deified, and become cult objects. On the other hand, there are a lot of machines that are created . . . for no reason; here we have machines-crafts, all kinds of bizarre mechanisms, devices, models of 'eternal movers' and so on. In contrast to machines created for a reason as a part of technological progress, useless machines are created (or rather are not-quite-created and constantly re-created) without any reference to their 'usefulness' and productivity. Their time of birth is the future, their place – the Master's powerful imagination. Their true home-land is in the future. The avant-garde consciousness needs precisely such fantastic machines: it needs to capture the future and topple it with one push into the present, to present it as a given.

The general notion of the Machine can be split into classes. The split would be done on the basis of questions such as the following: What kind of energy and material of Nature (Cosmos) is used and how? From which 'working parts' are machines assembled? What set of initial functions do they have? And so on.

Here are the resulting classes:

First class: technical machines; a large group of machines (mechanical, hydraulic, electrical, electronic and so on). Such machines are exemplars of technical devices, and are, properly speaking, machines by definition.

Second class: social machines (this class includes pedagogical-orthopaedic, medical, panoptic or surveillance machines, bureaucratic, militaristic, terroristic, imperial-territorial and other similar kinds of machines).

Third class: biomachines or organic machines, reproductive machines (self-replicating machines, such as, above all, living organisms).

Fourth class: machines that do not belong to any of the mentioned classes of machines; these are 'in-between' machines, dream-like, imaginary, virtual machines; these are fantastical machines (literary, theatrical, architectural and so on) that are not susceptible to representation. It is a kind of machinic or machinised unconscious; these machines are idle, neutered, ruined, but overwhelmed by desire: moving from negation of what is desired to its affirmation (a jump from a minus to a plus of the desire). Deleuze and Guattari called these machines *machines désirantes* – desiring-machines. These machines are ancient and primitive, for comparison they should be linked to the images of the Proto-machine. Platonov often pits these two machines against each other – on the one side, there is the ideal, technically perfect Machine, on the other, the archaic and oppressive Proto-machine (as in *The Foundation Pit*) – in order to reinforce, in my view, the contradiction in the avant-garde vision of the future and its tragic insolvability: the struggle to the death between machines. The revolutionary machine of Platonov's *Chevengur* is beautiful and consists of several working parts: Rosa Luxemburg's 'grave' – Revolution – Horse (named 'Natural Force') – Rider (cavalryman Kopenkin) – Steppe. But an electromagnetic resonator is also beautiful and revolutionary since it produces the current from natural light.

Images of the Machine: A Short Synopsis

It is important to answer the question regarding the reproduction of the avant-garde Machine. As soon as we begin to study its organisation, the main 'working' element comes to the forefront; it is, as it were, the essence of the machinic action itself. The original, autopoietic elements in the machinism of the avant-garde were the following: architekton (Malevich), 'dynamo-machine' (Nikolas Tesla and Andrei Platonov), Gestalt (Ernst Jünger), modulator (Le Corbusier), attraction (Eisenstein), Rodchenko's 'extreme angles (of vision)', and even Velemir Khlebnikov's numerical 'gamma of history'. In sum, at the centre of the early avant-garde – the time of 'Sturm und Drang' – there was a machine, and we need to understand its presence from the point of view of the revolution with which it was identified.

Platonov could not imagine a successful outcome for a revolution without a machine that replaced nature, subjecting it to a radical rework. The avant-garde machine refers to the machines of the future, machines that overcome the future. Therefore, it is often defined as the machine that annihilates time. An experience of life opens up in which time is produced just like everything else. Visibility, accessibility, size, reproduction of the world's things – all these are under the control of the Master, who senses and thinks like a machine. The machine provokes the new experience of the senses by eliminating hard manual labour, by creating a new order of necessary sensations and experiences. A revolutionary thrust into a new state of (radically renewed) existence is instantaneous, and only a machine is capable of such a thrust forward. Malevich attempted to express this, perhaps with more force than other avant-garde artists. What is being reworked with the help of the machine? Above all, the human body:

> An armoured tool, a car represents a small example of what I have been saying. If a man sitting in it is still separate from it, it is because this particular body that man has put on cannot fulfil all functions. The man himself, as a technical organ, can fulfil all the functions necessary for his soul, and therefore the soul lives within him and leaves him when the functions are no longer fulfilled: if a car could perfectly fulfil all man's needs, he would never leave it. The features of the latter are found in a greater solution: for example, the hydroplane. Air and water are contained in it, and when everything has been provided for, man will leave his new body no more.[8]

---

8   Kazimir Malevich, 'God Is Not Cast Down', in *Essays on Art, Volume 1: 1915–1928*, trans. Xenia Glowacki-Prus and Arnold McMillin, ed. Troels Andersen, Copenhagen: Borgen, 1968, 220 [188–223].

When humanity achieves unity – it is on the path now – it must unite with the new world which has flown out of its skull: with the organisms with which he is at present engaged in a bloody struggle. The pilot conducts unending war with his aeroplane: he wants to overcome it and to graft onto himself this new-grown body, to fuse it inseparably with his organism: the operation must be conducted with pain and blood so long as we consist of bones, flesh and blood.[9]

The church is striving through its religion to bring man's consciousness to God, as perfection, whilst the materialist is striving to attain perfection in the machine as self-nourishment: the one intends to nourish himself with God, the other with a machine.[10]

The techno-environment – 'machines' – is part of the human experience of the body that can no longer be itself. According to Malevich, the main moment of de-anthropologisation of the world is *speed*:

Speed is our essence, and each day we strive to run faster: our consciousness has now exceeded our comprehension. As a result, we are becoming sensitive to the perception of a new construction expressing the force of dynamism. Every machine is a phenomenon representing consciousness of speed, and every revelation of new speed of whatever kind it may be, leads us directly to the discovery of a real sign. Futurism and Cubism are great experiments within a natural development, thanks to which the future and our modern world are born. When our consciousness comprehends the great importance of speed in movement it will produce corresponding new forms.[11]

The machine is the new skin, the new, more sensitive intermediary, with the help of which new experiences and sensations are born; the machine is the rapid transformation of the nearest and the farthest realm of human habitat.

Malevich interprets his supremacist squares primarily as exemplars (along with architektons and tables). But what are these 'squares of

9   Malevich, 'On New Systems in Art', in *Essays on Art, Volume 1*, 107 [83–117].

10   Malevich, 'God Is Not Cast Down', 211.

11   Malevich, 'The Question of Imitative Art', in *Essays on Art, Volume 1*, 180 [165–82].

squares'? Are they not a 'zero-point of meaning', an 'original ideal' or an 'original copy'? The black square is not painting, but a tool of painting, if you like, an exemplar with which to modify any object of painting. The imitative, the architectural, the sculptural – the artistic itself has become a craft that participates in the revolutionary reorganisation of the world. If we take Malevich's square to be an example of a complete experience of avant-gardism, then that is precisely what one refers to as *tabula rasa*. It is the most primitive machine of painting, painting of modernity (I would even call it the machine of the avant-garde). Each 'square' consists of squares nested into one another – one large, the other small – the play between them taking place on the same grid of relationships (occupied/ unoccupied, full/empty, dark/light). This is the recreation of an ancient and primitive machine of painting and the goal of the avant-garde. The meaning is given only to what can be used to create the Work (of art), but not the Work itself, because otherwise there would be no need for any intermediary tool. In modernity and modernism, the meaning of the work of art still makes sense in the general strategy of Mimesis, but in the avant-garde vision of the world we see the victory of Mathesis. A dehumanised reality is the ecstasy of the Machine (Marinetti).[12] The constructing, mechanising, geometric reason serves this ecstasy. An entire collection of new projective instruments of painting is nothing compared to the project itself, the architekton, which represents the endless reproduction of Creation.

Is this not what Fernand Léger and Le Corbusier – those faithful sons of machinism – were talking about? For both, the machine is what establishes the order and what cannot be dispersed and dissolved; on the contrary, it collects, consolidates, creates completed unities. Le Corbusier, in one of the industrial projects, directly links the idea of a new factory ('the green factory' – *l'usine verte*) with the creation of a machine of machines, i.e. the organisation of the entire cycle of production from the position of some completed perfect order.

---

12   Cf. 'We declare that the world's splendour has been enriched by a new beauty; the beauty of speed. A racing motor-car, its frame adorned with great pipes, like snakes with explosive breath . . . a roaring motor-car, which looks as though running on shrapnel, is more beautiful than the Victory of Samothrace' (F. T. Marinetti, 'Initial Manifesto of Futurism', in *Exhibition of Works by the Italian Futurist Painters*, London: The Sackville Gallery, 1912, 3).

The machines carry out the exaggeration of all human gestures often to the point of the grimace: grinding and crushing, pounding, rolling, stretching, blowing and hammering. So much gesticulation creates an impression. At times, slowness of giants; huge drop hammers, huge presses; at other times, dangerous speeds of snakes or lightnings, galloping and gliding; everywhere are fantastical or maniacal limbs with their sinister gestures.[13]

Instead of this industrial hell of the 'black factory', the new 'green' factory is a perfectly organised, harmonious and humanised space of production:

In the 'green factory' the labour process will once again take place under the 'condition of nature'. The sun, the space and the greenery will bring here, as into the residential quarters, the connection with the cosmos, the response to the pulsations of lungs, the virtue of fresh air, as well as the presence of the natural environment that previously presided over the long and meticulous development of the human being.[14]

The machinic world that replaces the old industrial epochs brings with it a new aesthetic sensation: the machine is the object of imitation; one wants to become a machine. The machine becomes the decisive factor in the formation of a new environment (including a new artistic environment). Léger develops the idea of the 'architecture of the mechanical'.[15] The machine is now one of the universal aesthetic objects. Moreover, the human is now captured in the dynamics of machinic mimesis. Léger paints his canvases in a machinic style; he sees and feels the organic and the natural as if he were a machine. We find something similar, expressed with a higher degree of radicalism, in the architecture of Le Corbusier, with his attempt to introduce the smallest architectural-anthropometric unit: the modulor, 'a harmonic measure to the human scale, universally applicable to architecture and mechanics'.[16] And elsewhere: 'This

---

13   Le Corbusier, *Les trois établissements humains*, Paris: Éditions Denoël, 1945, 176–7.

14   Ibid., 178.

15   Fernand Léger, *Functions of Painting*, trans. Alexandra Anderson, New York: Viking Press, 1973, 53. A large section of Léger's book is devoted to the machine aesthetic. 'The machine is dressed up and has become a spectacle . . .' (ibid., 55).

16   Le Corbusier, *Œuvre complète en 8 volumes, Volume 5: 1946–1952*, Zurich: Les Editions d'Architecture, 1953, 179.

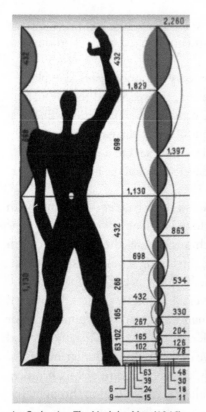 

Le Corbusier, *The Modulor Man* (1946)   Fernand Léger, *Mechanical Elements* (1924)

time, it was a simple matter to give a description: the "Modulor" is a measuring tool based on the human body and on mathematics. A man-with-arm-upraised provided, at the determining points of his occupation of space – foot, solar plexus, head, tips of fingers of the upraised arm – three intervals which give rise to a series of golden sections, called the Fibonacci series.'[17] A particular human dimensionality, alienated from particular human individuals, becomes the standard for determining a method for living. To some extent, cities-utopias with their ideal organ-isation of collective life, as imagined by Campanella, Thomas More, Fourier and Bentham, are close to what Le Corbusier later called 'the machine for housing'.[18] We can trace a clearer difference between the technical machine and the social machine, and then the social machine and the aesthetic, imaginary machine, and then between all these and the biomachine, on the basis of the avant-garde model of machinism.

Film-camera/photo-camera are the necessary conditions for the new machinised view of the world; at the beginning of the century, they still appear alienated from the previous form of perception. Thus, Rodchen-ko's famous 'extreme-angle technique' aims to find positions for filming where the apparatus would no longer depend on the human perspective and would film what we would otherwise be unable to see (or would see completely differently).

The angle of filming became more complicated and varied. But its connection to the human eye, with its usual perspective of vision, has not been interrupted. However, this connection is not necessary.

---

17   Le Corbusier, *The Modulor: A Harmonious Measure to the Human Scale Univer-sally Applicable to Architecture and Mechanics*, trans. Peter de Francia and Anna Bostock, New York: Faber and Faber, 1954, 55.

18   To be sure, Le Corbusier's ideas have been repeatedly challenged and criticised rather harshly. Some influential scientists have seen in them an expression of an overly simplistic and mechanised view of life. For example, Pierre Francastel expressed his atti-tude in a sharp form: 'Le Corbusier's universe is that of concentration camps. At best, it is the ghetto. Let me again stress that my intent is not to make Le Corbusier into a propagan-dist on the order of Pétain and Hitler, men whose hands are stained with slime and blood.' Le Corbusier, in his view, 'saw the creation of dwelling "cells" as the key to human happi-ness'. Each apartment is a 'honeycomb' or a 'cell'; one number of them forms a dwelling, another an institution, or a place of work; their common unity of inhabitation forms the city as a whole, and cities in turn constitute the Universum. The avant-garde machines are taking us back to the utopias of the Enlightenment. See Pierre Francastel, *Art and Tech-nology in the Nineteenth and Twentieth Centuries*, New York: Zone Books, 2000, 52, 53.

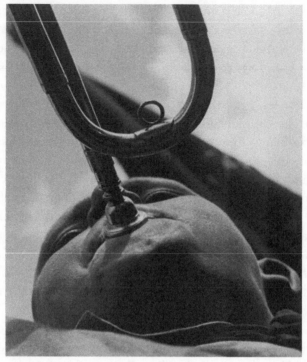

Rodchenko, *Pioneer-trumpeter* (1930)

Moreover, it needlessly restricts the possibilities of the filming apparatus. The apparatus can operate independently. It can see in a way that a
person is not used to. It may suggest its own point of view.[19]

The ability of the cinematographer (or the photographer) to machinise
the process of filming (or shooting) comes to the fore. Here, there is not
yet any irony, any scepticism, any hatred that someone like Wilhelm
Reich directed at contemporary technocracy, i.e. all these 'experiences'
of technical progress that later made the revolutionary utopia into the
subject matter of anti-utopian novels (Zamyatin, Huxley, Platonov).[20]

---

19   Osip Brik, 'Chego ne vidit glaz' [What the eye doesn't see], *Sovetskoe kino* 2
(1926), 23 (cited in A.N. Lavrentiev, *Rakursy Rodchenko* [Rodchenko's extreme angles],
Moscow, 1992, 62).

20   An anti-utopia is a political satire and science-fiction, where the author delib-
erately debunks illusions about a 'technologically beautiful' future. Platonov's works do
not fall within this core category, for in them there are no references to a 'real' future, but
to an apocalyptic, intensely experienced anticipation of the End and the Beginning of
the New World (but not the future itself). His anti-utopia is outside of time and history.

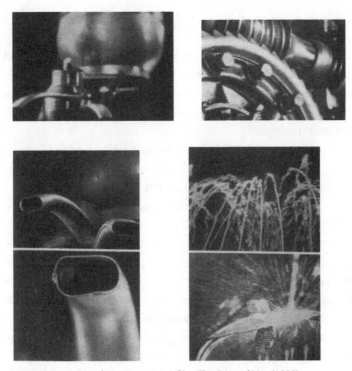

Separator-machine from Eisenstein's film *The General Line* (1929)

In the early 'avant-garde' cinema of Sergei Eisenstein, we find 'machines-attractions': factory tools and mechanisms (in *Strike*), a battleship (in *Battleship Potemkin*), a separator (in *The Old and the New*). The mechanics of attraction is used to produce certain effects, their action on the viewer must be technically predictable. For example, a machine-separator acts as a machine of love and unity, an ecstatic collective machine. There are two aspects to consider here: on the one hand, the ecstatic field around the separator is subject to machinic rhythm, and this rhythm is used to organise the collective economy, so that its members cease to be private owners and are transformed, in one blow, into collectivists; on the other hand, the 'separator' is a particular technical device, represented as the Machine (of all machines), with an amazing mechanical constitution, alienated from human beings, and with a brilliant form that resembles the ancient Grail. The machine-separator is something radically new and at the same time something radically ancient. Properly speaking, the accelerated rotation of the machine prepares a future orgy, a future orgasmic explosion. For Eisenstein, the most powerful manifestation of machinism was connected precisely with such sexual tension, with the incredible power that the Machine inspired in its initial adepts-inventors. The clear and clean rhythm, the inevitability of repetition, the inexhaustible energy, and, finally, the result itself achieved with such ease. Such perception of the machine was to be expected, although it was prompted by *another* machine – the film camera that directly affected the viewing masses' imagination.

The stunning success of Vertov's *The Man with a Movie Camera* shows that the film camera has become the great social machine. We see how it assembles reality (its accidental fragments) into a single mosaic whole, despite the fact that these fragments were captured individually in their own dimensions. Now, things that were removed from one another, that could never intersect in reality, are found next to each other, have become close and comparable; they can now be perceived with one movement of one's gaze, in one time and in one form of reality. This gaze is born of a film camera and is artificial, machinic and dehumanised. The effect of the film was precisely in the technological equipment of the film subject. The programme of 'Kino-Eye': the subject must literally and physically coincide with the 'eye' of the film camera. But Eisenstein's approach is different – it is not so much about the alienations of the visible (this was the intention of Vertov's experiment), but about the engagement of mass consciousness in the visible for a particular purpose; not a disinterested gaze of cognition, but a complete inclusion of the viewer in machinic ecstasy. Here the film camera performs the function of translating one state of consciousness into another, i.e. it is the main tool of control of mass consciousness.

1

Positions of Reading

To See – Not to Understand

When we read Platonov, initially nothing else is required, we just read, we are enchanted. But now we stop to take a breath, to check again whether we are reading correctly. Is it the piercing veracity of *Epifan Locks*, *Makar the Doubtful*, *Chevengur* and *The Foundation Pit* that mystifies us and draws us into a world that cannot be either accepted or forgiven? Perhaps even the knowledge of Soviet history cannot improve our understanding of these texts? The doubts would be justified if the literary world created by Platonov were a glimpse, a reflection, of another, historically limited world, a document that in its own language provides a witness to the era of Stalin's industrialisation and collectivisation, to the fate of the Russian village of the 1920s and 1930s. But our reading of Platonov does not depend on the desire to know how it really was, and his prose is far from revealing to us the 'blank spots' of our country's history.[1] Nevertheless,

---

1   When the time of action of the utopian 'new life' ends, which is somewhere from the beginning to the middle of 1920s, Platonov writes a number of fantastical novels: *Happy Moscow*, *Technical Novel*, *Chevengur*, *The Juvenile Sea* and *The Foundation Pit* (all written around the same time); these are generally classified as 'anti-utopias' (along with Zamyatin's *We*, Alexei Tolstoy's *Aelita* and Huxley's *Brave New World*). What are these novels about? Are they about the great technological inventions that humanity is on the verge of discovering, or about the future that has come without changing anything, and that turned out to be the great social catastrophe that no one can survive without loss? The post-revolutionary energy is accumulating and preparing to embark on the path of

literature sometimes provides much more than historical research, presenting the scene of history in its genuine dramatism.

During the first moments of reading, we are captured by two equally active distances: one *removes* what we read from us, let us call it the *comic* distance; the other, on the contrary, *brings it closer* to us, and this is the *tragic* distance. In the process of reading, we cannot actively choose one or the other. We discover them later, as if *post festum*. We can choose one of them only by refusing the other. In the process of reading, it is impossible to choose, because we must simply read, and not choose, i.e. be a part of the topology of the world that is already established. The entire effect is in the play of distances. It is difficult to avoid a condescending sneer, and at times we are bound to let out a hearty laugh, when we listen to the 'ridiculous', 'illiterate', almost insane speeches of Platonov's characters. On the other hand, there is a sense of hopelessness in the face of the outright irrationality and cruelty of a world where death roams freely, taking on unexpected disguises, and where the dead and the living are equal in their rights. At each moment of reading, we encounter one and the same distance that, by making us independent of what we read, or by making us into judges of what we read, immediately returns us along an invisible arc to our own selves. Now we are the object of provocation, disgust and longing. 'All this is funny! Pure comedy!' But to say this is to assume that what is read can be evaluated, that it is easy to distance oneself from it (even if with the sense of loss). But such stratification cannot be accomplished. The reading is continuous. The emotional-sensuous atmosphere remains the same; we are denied the right to choose – there is no joy without pain, or laughter without longing. And we move, jumping and spinning, now moving away from, now moving closer to what we are reading; one distance is hiding in the other. The old formula: Gogol's laughter through tears (that are 'invisible to the world'). A precisely aimed 'shock' comedy makes us seek an emotional shelter in a tragic experience (the same worrying sense of belonging to a national tragedy). It is well known that where comedy is intrusive, coercive, it easily turns into fear and becomes torture. Having only one, purely laugher-based principle is unthinkable for Platonov's literature. That is why to read Platonov is to

---

final sacrifice and loss. Almost every novel by Platonov describes the impossibility of recovering the lost energy of life. That is why it seems that now it is the machine that should be better able to conserve and distribute the energy that human beings spend for nothing and lose in wars, crimes and in the fight against Nature.

experience a complex feeling, where the comic is inseparable from the tragic, where we are forced to suffer and to laugh. And the reason for this is the *omnipresent* guide we have to trust, a certain unnamed character in Platonov's literature who sees everything, knows everything, but remains silent. It gets given strange names such as 'dead brother' or 'eunuch of the soul'. In *Chevengur*, we find the following explanation:

> But there is within man also a tiny spectator who takes part neither in action nor in suffering, and who is always cold-blooded and the same. It is his service to see and be a witness, but he is without franchise in the life of man and it is not known why he exists in solitude. This corner of man's consciousness is lit both day and night, like the doorman's room in a large building. This heart doorman sits entire days at the entrance into man and knows all the inhabitants of his building, but not a single resident asks the doorman's advice about his affairs. The residents come and go while the spectator-doorman watches them with his eyes. His powerless knowledge of everything makes him sometimes seem sad, but he is always polite, distant, and he keeps an apartment in another building. In the event of fire, the doorman telephones the firemen and watches further events from without.
>
> While Dvanov walked and rode without memory, this spectator within him saw everything, but it never warned him and never helped him, not once. He lived parallel to Dvanov, but he wasn't Dvanov.
>
> He existed somewhat like a man's dead brother; everything human seemed to be at hand, but something tiny and vital was lacking. Man never remembers him, but always trusts him, just as when a tenant leaves his house and his wife within, he is never jealous of her and the doorman. This is the eunuch of man's soul.[2]

It is this 'eunuch of the soul' who, due to his special qualities as an observer, creates for us a third distance, which, including the intense opposition of the two preceding ones (tragedy and comedy), is a distance not of experience but of *pure vision*. The entire field of vision has been transformed: the *eunuch of the soul* becomes the main character who is claiming to have more than a universal, pure and 'unblinking' gaze. The new position, the position of the eunuch of the soul, is no longer the

---

2   Andrei Platonov, *Chevengur*, trans. Anthony Olcott, Ann Arbor: Ardis, 1978, 80.

position of the human eye, even if it is improved or adequately prepared; the eunuch's gaze sees, but does not desire what it sees, it is a fleshless eye outside the body, and perhaps even standing against the body. It is important to remember that the eunuch of the soul is not only a part of Dvanov but is able to become a completely independent character (like Pukhov in the novel *The Innermost Man*). 'Dvanov however did not know what is preserved and guarded within the body of each man, while Prokofy knew almost exactly, and so was extremely suspicious of a silent man.'[3] The uninterrupted exchange of places between the main character and the 'eunuch of the soul' creates a situation where the two become indistinguishable. The comedy of fact resonates here with the identity of the 'eunuch of the soul' and the author's consciousness. Here the longing consciousness ends, and the despair begins. The preceding contemplative experience is rejected in favour of the new observer who contemplates the world from the 'heights of socialism'.[4]

Machine for the Eye

> I am Kino-Eye, I am a mechanical eye.
> I, a machine, show you the world
> as only I can see it.[5]

In Platonov's early essay entitled 'Proletarian Poetry' and in a fragment called 'On Love' we find very important statements without which it would be difficult to explain the optical constructions of works such as *The Foundation Pit*, *Chevengur* and *The Juvenile Sea*. The first position for the eye: 'The point of objective, independent observation', writes Platonov,

---

3   Ibid., 268.

4   Cf. 'If we further label this traveller as ourselves (using the "I"), it is only for briefness of speech, and not because we admit that weak contemplation is more important than tension and struggle. On the contrary, in our time, a roaming observer is something very small, a half-creature, for he is not a direct participant in the cause of communism. And further, the real observer who sees true things cannot exist in our time outside of labour and proletarian order, for valuable observation can only come from the experience of the hard work of building the socialist system' (Andrei Platonov, 'Vprok. Bedniatskaia khronika' [For future use: A poor peasant's chronicle], in *Efirnyi trakt* [The ethereal tract], Moscow, 2011, 285).

5   Dziga Vertov, *Kino-Eye: The Writings of Dziga Vertov*, ed. Annette Michelson, trans. Kevin O'Brien, Berkeley: University of California Press, 1984, 17.

'coincides with the centre of a perfect organisation. Only by moving away from the world and from oneself can one see that there is all this and what all this wants to be.'[6] What is this point of observation and who is found in it? Platonov provides an answer: this position of observation is taken by a special eye, an 'eye of science' as he calls it, an 'unblinking eye of humanity', a 'light that is pure and transparent, but neither warm nor cold'.[7] The new vision, where it can achieve a perfect organisation, will 'automatically' change the world itself, the matter of the world in which 'the notions of work, resistance, matter, humanity and so on, will certainly not exist'.[8] In the position of the 'eunuch of the soul' there is one peculiarity: the eye of the eunuch of the soul welcomes emptiness, it sees only intervals, ruptures, gaps, apertures of the visible world, and through them it sees flickering surfaces, 'far away distances', disappearing horizons, grey mirages, the monotony of the deserted, depleted landscapes of the steppe. It is as if it sees nothing, because its vision is focused on what cannot be visible but is the condition of visibility. We recognise a shape by separating it from the background; the background itself remains invisible, but we 'see' it with the help of a figure that gives it meaning. The background itself is inert and faceless. Platonov, however, wants to make us trust the eunuch of the soul who is enchanted by the emptiness of the background.

Let us try to represent this as a diagram:

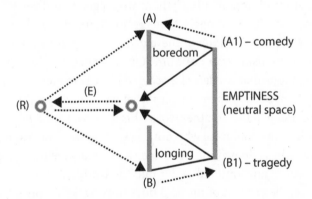

6   Andrei Platonov, 'Proletarskaya poeziia' [Proletarian poetry], in *Sochinenia, Tom pervyi, 1918–1927, Kniga vtoraya* [Works, Volume 1: 1918–1927, Book Two], Moscow, 2004, 163–4.

7   Andrei Platonov, 'O lyubvi' [On love], in *Krasnyi Platonov* [Red Platonov], Moscow, 2006, 252.

8   Platonov, 'O kul'ture zapryazhennogo sveta i poznannogo elektrichestva' [On the culture of harnessed light and cognised electricity], in *Krasnyi Platonov*, 247.

We read Platonov with the help of this *optical* machine. The point (R) is the *reader*; the point (E) is the eunuch of the soul. They are centres of two spaces, as if located inside one another. The point (E) is the most important point in the diagram since that is where the reader encounters the realities of Platonov's world. It is a shocking point that creates an effect of *making-strange*. The very first contact creates an instant flash of emotions, an affect is transformed into a *distance*. If the affect is cognised as a *tragedy* – despair, compassion and pain – then the distance will be determined by a process of *moving closer*, by the growing significance of figures-characters (who go beyond the literary space); the experience is projected into the text and then extracted as an image that corresponds to the emotional transition along the line (B – B^1 – R). The amplitude of the tragic experience is formed in point (R), not in (E), i.e. it is *secondary* in relation to the feeling of shock experienced by the reader during the first moments of reading.

An analogous procedure of emotionally loaded reaction operates at the level of the *comic* effect. With one distinction: now the reader is not moving closer, but moving away, and the faster he moves away, the more noticeable is the comic nature of situation along the line (A – A^1 – R). The tragedy disappears, and the imposing figures of meaning, suffering and pain are reduced to tiny figurines, originating from the Russian revolutionary tradition of 'lubok'; these are poignant and very funny figurines ('they speak so strangely, they are so thoughtful and smart'). For the eunuch of the soul, none of these distances is primary, the eunuch's point of view is *outside of any distance*. One distance is hiding in another; they are positions that will later be occupied by the reader. The eunuch of the soul cannot occupy them; he sees what we cannot see, the emptiness itself, the *nothing* of life. In other words, his gaze controls a *neutral* space. The eunuch of the soul is he who observes, witnesses, moves in parallel; by definition, he is denied the right to be a normally feeling being, much less to introduce any 'rational' order into the world.

Of course, the eunuch of the soul does not always simply see: a sharp change in the realm of observed events takes place simultaneously with the appearance of a previously repressed emotional relation (sometimes it is empathy, more often it is grief and longing). It is precisely at this point that his path curves, the parallel lines converge in one point, and that point is almost always death. Only death can revive important vital functions, and it revives them only once, immediately erasing them from memory.

Encountering the inconsistencies in the functions of observation, the reader begins to understand that what he reads, though inspired by the eunuch of the soul, does not depend on his ways of observation. Platonov's prose lives in a constantly recreated gap between the experience and the form of representation controlled by the eunuch of the soul. Let us pay attention! Perhaps the most important thing here is that the eunuch of the soul is unable to feel what he observes; it is precisely the radical commitment to describe but to will nothing that determines the peculiarity of this attitude.

The observer's spiritual poverty creates a field of negative corporeal signs that actively influence the process of reading. But we should not forget that the eunuch of the soul is a remnant of the 'soul', perhaps its 'part'. Perhaps it is a creature that survived a terrible fear of castration; there's pain and the shame of punishment (a threat coming from the Father-Despot). And yet his position is *objective*; it is the position of an asexual being whose consciousness is not clouded by various desires and therefore remains neutral toward human passions. The eunuch of the soul looks out, keeps an eye, on all the bodies, and then immediately 'sticks' itself to the bodies that are ready to desire.

Thus, 'the eunuch of the soul' is the subject (E) with a soul, but this soul is emotionally limited by a vision of a neutral space: along the line $(E - A^1)$ we get the leading emotion, the general tonality of emotion, which is the reaction to the *neutral* space; it is the emotion of *boredom*. Whoever reads Platonov has been warned about this. Along the line $(E - B^1)$ we get another emotion, which is equally active during our reading, the emotion of *longing*. Behind this split into tragedy and comedy we find the possibility of transition between three emotional states: *boredom – longing – emptiness*. The eunuch of the soul is not an emotionless observer, though he does declare his objectivity; he sees the world in one tonality.

I will give two examples, which I hope will clarify our scheme from the position of special knowledge.

(1) *The catastrophe of perception.* As we read Platonov, we come closer and closer to defining our experience as *a catastrophe of perception*. Let us recall the old textbook example of the psychology of perception: *an antique vase* and *two profiles*. Psychologists say that the perception of this picture is distinguished by *bistability*, because in one case we can

say 'what we see is a *vase*', and in the other case 'we see two *profiles*'. The subordination of the figure and the background is broken. The figure does not stand against the background, because its contour is constructed, or, more precisely, cut from the background itself, and in such a way that its external borders are lines that also belong to another figure. What is most interesting here is the dynamics of switching perception. How do we move from one discrete image to another? Yes, indeed, 'it is a vase', but then in the next moment it is no longer a vase, but two profiles. By naming what we see, we switch from one space to another, and this switch depends on identifying the figure and on naming it. In other words, if I identified something with something that is known to me, then I perceived it. I perceive only by pointing out what must be perceived.

The normal course of perception is disturbed, because we cannot move smoothly from one image to another; there is a rupture between them. An essential ontological difference. Two strategies that are artificially combined, each lacking the most basic element: the ability to get rid of another image's boundary. To see the profiles, one needs to trace with one's eyes the boundaries of the vase; to see the vase – the boundaries of the profiles. The distinguishing line is the same and is equal to itself precisely when it simultaneously belongs to both figures at the same time: being *outside* one figure, it is at the same time *inside* the other figure. This curve is where the boundary of a perceptive catastrophe passes, and this line must be interpreted as a topological boundary (not as a geometric one) that separates only insofar as it connects. That is the essence of the phenomenon of the catastrophe of perception. For a time, we are experiencing something similar to a shock, unable to synthesise a single image, Gestalt. And that means that our perception of the world is *discrete*: a time between two figures passed but was not perceived (I mean the instant of the switch between them). The transition from one figure to another is instantaneous and destructive, but topologically smooth and continuous.[9]

(2) *Dziga Vertov and the interval.* The ideal of Platonov's vision is in solidarity with Dziga Vertov's experiments in cinematography. How is it possible to see matter? Or, perhaps, how can matter see itself? These questions can be made more precise: how and by what means is it possible to see what remains invisible (the material composition of the world at the level of microscopy of forces and elements)? The invention of cinematography (the ideal technical means of cognising the world) was an incredibly inspiring event for many avant-garde figures. Vertov created the theory of a 'superhuman eye'. This *machine-eye* (cinematic-eye, kino-eye) was a wonderful exemplar of optical mechanics: 'The kino-eye lives and moves in time and space; it gathers and records impressions in a manner wholly different from that of the human eye. The position of our bodies while observing or our perception of a certain number of features of a visual phenomenon in a given instant are by no means obligatory limitations for the camera which, since it is perfected, perceives more and better.'[10] It is only by means of this mechanical eye that a human being is connected to a new vision that is able to see 'without limits and distances'. And for that, the kino-eye has many possibilities: some are determined by the specificity of the camera as a mechanical-optical device (its ability to generate new points of view on the world); others are determined by montage, which makes it possible to combine different positions of the camera in time and space, to connect what cannot be connected: far and near, great and unnoticeable, random and expected.[11]

---

9   For example, the surreal experience of René Magritte was found precisely in this use of the effect of bistability of perception.

10   Vertov, *Kino-Eye*, 15.

11   In the 1920s, Vertov puts forward his theory of the use of tracking ('travelling') shots, as well as 'top-down' and 'bottom-up' angles (together with Rodchenko), all sorts of speed-ups and delays, even the introduction of a 'subjective camera'. Here we see a sharp difference in attitudes: for Vertov everything turns out to be visible in the motion of the kino-eye, and this motion is sped-up and forced; speed allows one to be everywhere, in the very midst of life; it allows one to get ahead of the event, to open it up, to create it. On the contrary, there is no joy of motion in Platonov; there is nothing that is

We see the emergence of unusual new spaces for the human eye to see; limited by its perceptive prejudices, the eye finds all of this quite shocking. The principle of an 'interval' allows for a combination of the possibilities of the camera's mechanical eye and the technique of montage. The camera captures reality from unusual angles, one point of view is separated from another by an interval (either a temporal or a spatial one). The interval does not restrict the movement of the camera, but gives it an opportunity to show the invisible, to penetrate into the depths of the material world. A sequence of intervals organises the rhythm of the visible; the montage only expresses these rhythms.[12] For example, Vertov's film, *A Sixth Part of the World*, is an attempt to create the conditions for the formation of a common supranational identity. In other words, the eye is endowed with superhuman meaning, it becomes a *kino-eye*; it is not just a technical means, but the eye of matter itself, with which it can see itself in a state, place and time where there is no place for human perception. This previously unseen content shocks us. New strategies of montage are able to reduce random oscillations of intervals in space and time to a single rhythm of the material whole. A path to creating new bodies and worlds is now open. In this sense, communism is not so much a new social formation as a new form of universal organisation of matter. Indeed, when Vertov presents the nature of a mechanical eye ('film-camera') as a special organ of 'sense-perception', he means its 'non-human' properties. It is the eye of the mechanism, the eye-machine. In other words, it stands against human corporeality and does not need it, i.e. it exists outside the limitations usually imposed on the process of seeing by the parameters of the human body. Why do we mention Vertov's use of experiments here? Because Platonov's vision also rests on the possibility of an *intervalisation* of the visible. But Platonov's interval should be understood not as something that connects all that is disconnected in space and time, but

---

extremely fast; the world he describes has lost its taste for rhythm and speed; we always see a walking, stopping, falling and lying body that is tired and stricken by the boredom of the world, as if by leprosy.

12   Cf. 'Intervals (the transitions from one movement to another) are the material, the elements of the art of movement, and by no means the movements themselves. It is they (the intervals) which draw the movement to a kinetic resolution. The organisation of movement is the organisation of its elements, or its intervals, into phrases. In each phrase there is a rise, a high point, and a falling off (expressed in varying degrees) of movement. A composition is made of phrases, just as a phrase is made of intervals of movement' (Vertov, *Kino-Eye*, 8–9).

as an unfilled, 'empty' segment of space or as a paused 'interrupted' time. The energy of the interval in Platonov is represented by the energy of emptiness, desolation or devastation of space.

A broader framework is needed to clarify the effect of the 'bistability of perception', which, in our opinion, is a consequence of the epochal sociogenesis. In the early 1920s, Platonov called for a point of view of 'objective independent observation', a position with the help of which one can not only see but also rebuild the entire matter of human and natural life. Later comes the figure of the *eunuch of the soul*, the symbol of the decline of the avant-garde's machinic utopias, for whom his own body, with which he ought to begin to explore the world, remains a strange empty house: it is no longer a 'mighty machine'. The unity of the observer and the observing 'I' disintegrates. The body, captured by the forces of the external (a cosmocratic utopia), is separated from the human subjectivity, from the 'soul'; it loses individual features. 'I myself, who am writing these words, have lived through a great epoch of thought, work and ruin, and nothing remains in me but a clairvoyant consciousness, and my heart feels nothing but only pumps blood.'[13] The new point of observation is now located not in an optimistic space of the will to rule over the world and nature, but in the realm of the catastrophic. The eunuch of the soul is the witness and the chronicler of the catastrophe. For Platonov, the catastrophe or the end of time, and generally the eschatological experience of time, was of enormous importance. That is how he experienced his time, like a time without time, like a time that seemed not to exist. How can one live in the present, if by the will of the greatest of the catastrophes, a revolutionary one, one suddenly finds oneself in the future where time no longer exists (where it disappeared like water in the sand)? The literatures of Dostoyevsky and Bely are apocalyptic in the sense that they live through every instant of the time that is coming to completion (the themes of 'suddenly-time' and 'blink-of-an-eye-time'). For Platonov, however, time *came to a standstill*, 'froze in a stupor', and one has to live as if the time really did end – one has to be 'after time', that is, dead. The heroes of *The Foundation Pit* tirelessly say: 'We are only suitable for the future if we are dead.' This epochal transition is best seen in the story 'The Descendants of the Sun', where it is done with the kind

---

13   Andrei Platonov, 'Potomki solntsa' [The descendants of the sun], in *Usomnivshy-isya Makar. Rasskazy 1920kh godov. Stikhotvoreniya.* [Makar the Doubtful. Short Stories from the 1920s. Poetry], Moscow, 2011, 332.

of power of sincerity and trust in the reader that Platonov subsequently
had to hide:

> I am a watchman and chronicler of a deserted globe. I am now the lone
> master of mountain peaks, plains and oceans. The ancient time has
> arrived on earth, any time now the glaciers will move south, and the
> birch trees will grow to the island of Ceylon.[14]

> Deep, quiet, thinking humanity. An army of machines, thundering,
> howling, full of concentrated might, in the orbit of electricity and fire,
> relentlessly and ruthlessly gnawing at matter.
>   Socialism is the power of the human thought on earth and every-
> where I see and will someday reach.
>   From tribes, states, classes, the climate catastrophe created a single
> humanity, with a single consciousness and a sleepless pace of work.
> The image of the death of life on earth gave people chaste brotherhood,
> discipline, heroism and genius.
>   The catastrophe had become the teacher and the leader of humanity,
> as it has always been. And because all future forces had to be concen-
> trated in the present – sexual and any other kind of love were destroyed.
> For if there is a power in the human body that can create a generation
> of workers for future times, the humankind has consciously stopped
> the workings of this power, so that it would work now, immediately,
> and not tomorrow.
>   And the human seed did not make children, but made the brain,
> grew and reinforced it – this was required by the deadly epoch of
> history.[15]

Now it is necessary to understand that only a miracle can balance out the
force of a catastrophe, only a miracle can return human time – a human
being can no longer do that; and it is a miracle of a *great machine* – the
future of humankind is in its hands.

---

14   Ibid., 329.
15   Ibid., 330–1.

A Dual Being: The Exterior and the Interior

That's the mystery of human evolution, that's why man has left all the other animals behind! What allowed him to carry it off was something trifling: he was able to train two feelings, two dark currents, to meet and measure their strength against each other . . . And meeting, they are transformed into human thought. Clearly, none of this is perceptible . . . Animals can experience these states too, but only occasionally and by chance. *But man has been nurtured by this same chance, he has become a dual being.*[16]

The gaze of the eunuch of the soul – is it not what we know today as the gaze of the schizo-subject? Let us test this hypothesis. A patient complains about the disconnectedness of his perceptions; thus, for example, he cannot find anything in common between the bird he sees and the same bird that he hears chirping: for him, these are two different birds, and there is a rupture between these two perceptions that makes him anxious. The bird starts to chirp only when the orders of the visible and the audible elements can be assigned to the same living being, to *this* bird. The patient cannot reduce the existence of his body and his representation of it to the same unified being, so he fears that *this body* is not his body, and that he may well do without it. We find something similar in the visual realm of the eunuch of the soul, who sees but does not grasp what is visible by discerning its essential functions; the most important element is missing in his vision, the evaluative-cognitive element. Emptiness becomes the main object of his contemplation, but it is a negative object that excludes understanding. Such vision is incapable of connecting disparate details into one non-contradictory picture. But the eunuch of the soul does not need to 'know' about what he sees. Platonov radically rejects the author-narrator's hidden position, the 'third point', the all-knowing and all-interpreting mediator, who alone can distinguish between the intertwined images of the comic and the tragic, the exterior and the interior, between figures and bodies, who alone can endow their interconnection with visibility and necessity. The eye of the eunuch of the soul sees only that which is *in between*, only that which can show

---

16   Andrey Platonov, *Happy Moscow*, trans. Robert and Elizabeth Chandler, New York: New York Review of Books, 2012, 59, emphasis in original.

the reader how to connect what cannot be connected. This is how the
separation of the *body* and the *soul* is made visible; no one lives in his
own body; the body only appears as something mortal. Why is it called
'dead brother', 'eunuch of the soul', 'midnight watchman', 'observer'? These
are Platonov's names for the strange homunculus who lives inside each
character's consciousness.

> All the same Dvanov lay down. It seemed to him that he was with
> someone else, that they saw at one and the same time both the lodging
> hut and Dvanov himself, lying on the stove. He moved over a bit to
> make room for his companion, embraced him, and slipped into
> oblivion.[17]

> Then Dvanov himself stopped in the thick of the weeds. Now he was
> not thinking of anything, and the old watchman in his mind kept the
> peace for his treasure. He would allow in only one visitor, who now
> was wandering about somewhere outside of thought. But she was not
> to be seen outside. An empty, muffled earth spread out before him,
> while a melting sun labored in the heavens like something dreary and
> artificial, and the people of Chevengur thought not of cannons but of
> one another. Then the watchman opened the rear door of memory and
> Dvanov again felt the warmth of consciousness in his head.[18]

> Dvanov lowered his head, consciousness lessened by the monotony of
> an even pace of motion, and what he felt now in his heart was a dam
> trembling continuously before the pressure of a rising lake of feelings.
> Feelings rose high against his heart, then tumbled down its other side,
> already transformed into a stream of mitigating thought. Still however
> the duty light of his watchman burned above the dam, the watchman
> who takes no part in the life of man, drowsing within him for a pittance
> of salary. Occasionally this light allowed Dvanov to see both expanses,
> the warm swelling sea of feelings and the long tumbling thought which
> ran down the dam, cooling itself with its own speed.[19]

---

17 Platonov, *Chevengur*, 82.
18 Ibid., 319.
19 Ibid., 120. Of course, Platonov was not the only one to use such language. Other
writers also used original and provocative literary styles: Andrei Bely, Alexei Remizov,

Here is another remarkable observation:

> And sometimes, in illness, in unhappiness, in love, in a terrible dream, at any moment, in fact, that's far removed from the normal, we clearly sense that there are two of us – that I am one person but there's someone else inside me as well. This someone, this mysterious 'he', often mutters and sometimes weeps, he wants to get out from inside you and go somewhere far away, he gets bored, he gets frightened . . . We can see there are two of us and that we've had enough of each other. We imagine the lightness, the freedom, the senseless paradise of an animal, when our consciousness was not dual but lonely. Only a moment separates us from the animals when we lose the duality of our consciousness, and very often we live in archaic times without understanding what that means . . . But then our two consciousnesses couple together again, we once again become human beings in the embrace of our 'two-edged' thought, and nature, organised according to the principle of impoverished singleness, grits her teeth and curls herself up to escape the activity of these terrible dual structures that she never engendered, that originated inside their own selves . . . I find it terrifying now to be on my own! These are two passions eternally copulating and warming my head . . .[20]

Despite being 'inside' a hidden greyish realm, the eunuch of the soul is *non-incarnate, not-in-the-flesh*: the body is separated from him and exists 'at a distance, not next to the flesh'. The hero's consciousness experiences something like a schizophrenic collapse. What is Dvanov (dva-nov, twofold)? A dream-like pair: Dvanov-I (father), Dvanov-II (son) derived from another primordial schizo-pair: Dvanov and the 'eunuch of the soul'. Platonov was subtly aware of the depth of this duality. All sensations that are recognised as authentic are located in a strange realm of 'I-sensation' that is not embodied, does not have any corporeal support, and therefore is unable to connect to the world by means of the necessary mediator,

---

Evgeny Zamyatin, Isaac Babel, Mikhail Bulgakov, Mikhail Zoshchenko, Ilya Ilf and Evgeni Petrov, Artem Vesely.

20   Platonov, *Happy Moscow*, 59–60. The splitting is presented here as the norm for the avant-garde revolutionary consciousness. The technique of making-strange moves to a different level. If Bely had it under control as if it were a chosen form of mimetic reactivity, even a game, then for Platonov there is nothing except this consciousness oppressed by the split.

which in this case is the image of the body. Moreover, what one today calls 'my body' is objectified in the external realm vis-à-vis the representation of the 'I-sensation' behind which hides a false, inauthentic subject. The body's organs, sensations and their functions are then perceived as foreign and as belonging to someone else. The schizo-subject observes them from the outside, even though he himself is located inside. What in the common practice of using the images of the body is designated as 'here' (*close*) and 'there' (*distant*) can in a schizophrenic clinical case be reversed: 'here' becomes 'there'. Dvanov is sent on a strange journey, for what he knows about himself, he knows from a silent watchman, a 'dead brother', who is supposedly his soul, but a non-incarnate soul, connected to a body double as to something random and defective. Dvanov continues to double at the expense of the eunuch of the soul. And calm and balance arrive only when he coincides with the father, or when he merges with the communal body of Chevengur.

As we can see in the diagram, the eunuch of the soul controls the space of a triangle defined by the solid line, i.e. everything that is 'above' or 'below' (tragedy/comedy are only interpretations). Can we say that this space is a *neutral* space? We can probably not find a more adequate term. The neutral space removes the liminal tension between the external and the internal, the distant and the near, one's own and the foreign, the tragic and the comic. The eunuch of the soul is able to see and 'feel' only because he is external to himself, and the more the space of the rupture increases, the more the interior becomes external to itself. The neutral space is the space where forces of the exterior form images of the interior. Indeed, the eunuch of the soul does not understand the organic, inherited connections of life. The eunuch of the soul often observes how some abandoned bodies bump into other abandoned bodies, how strange objects penetrate them, how they get stuck in the skin, interfere with breathing. Here is an example: small things – boxes, shards, felt boots, sweaters – suddenly transform into heavy objects of enormous volume and fall on Dvanov. 'He was obliged to let them enter into him; they fit snugly, pulling at his skin. Most of all Dvanov feared that his skin would burst. It wasn't animated, crushing objects that were terrifying, but rather that his skin might rip and that he would choke on the burning dry hairs of a felt boot stuck in the seams of his own skin.'[21] The skin no

---

21   Platonov, *Chevengur*, 89.

longer protects, it has ceased to be an insurmountable limit between the interior and the exterior. What was inside is now pushed to the surface of the skin; what was outside, turns out to be inside. And even though it is a dream, it is *real* as a sensation: the body becomes porous, covered with ruptures, loses the connection between 'I'-sensation (a 'corporeal I') and the body itself. The 'I-sensation' now travels all over its own body, and simply observes what happens to its bodily form without fear and surprise. Even the most thoughtful of Platonov's characters are more like wisemen-automatons than living and intelligent people responsible for their own actions. Therefore, they can observe their own physiology of thought, but are unable to master it psychologically. Physiology appears as something random, and they, these somnambular characters, these schizos, trapped in 'independent, objective observation', are doomed to remain strange natural automatons, whose consciousness flows along the surface of their own body and things, without finding refuge in the interior.

Platonov is fully conscious of this technique: the eunuch of the soul indeed 'knows neither corporeal nor spiritual pain'. It is because of this ignorance that none of his characters experience physical pain and suffering, it is a state of complete anaesthesia. Nevertheless, when we read Platonov, we cannot help but notice how a distant event somehow affects us deeply. The location of the pain's locus has shifted – now it is our interior realm. What is striking is not the accuracy of the indifferent description of a physical event, but rather the fact that the pain belongs to no one, as if Platonov's world is filled with forces that are blind to individual existence. And that is indeed the case . . . It is important to show not *this* physical pain, but the force that causes it. The sound of a deadly bullet, a cracking of bones from a punch, a deep wound (Dvanov's wound is 'a steel bird [which] had dug into the leg and was rustling the stinging edges of its wings'[22]) – all these are examples of something exterior that spreads itself over the surfaces of strange bodies, killing or maiming them, but these bodies themselves are not capable of feeling anything, there is no one to experience their pain. In other words, no one can question the power of external forces, and the eunuch of the soul is their first witness. Here are some examples:

---

22   Ibid., 71.

There he was once taken to the yard and put against a wall made of old fifteen-inch bricks; Bozhev had time to take a closer look at these old bricks, which still lie in ancient Russian fortresses, and he stroked them with his hand in his misfortune – and after Bozhev turned around, he was shot at. Bozhev felt the wind hitting him in the chest with a hard force, but could not fall into this force, even though he was already dead; all he did was slide down the wall.[23]

Here are the depictions of the execution of the 'bourgeoisie':

The Chekists shot their revolvers into the crowd of silent bourgeoisie, which had the day before taken communion, and the bourgeoisie fell clumsily and askew, twisting their greasy necks about so much it looked as though they might damage their spines. Each of them lost the power of his legs before he felt the wound, which allowed the slug to fall into its spot by chance and there grow over with living meat.[24]

Chepurny and Piyusya personally went to study the dead bourgeoisie. The dead lay in heaps of three, five or more, apparently having tried to draw together with at least parts of their bodies in these, their final moments of mutual separation. Chepurny tested the throats of the bourgeoisie with the back of his hand, just like engineers test the temperature of their bearings. It seemed to him that all the bourgeoisie were still alive . . .

Piyusya and Chepurny pinched all of the bourgeoisie and were not convinced of their decisive deadness. A few seemed still to be breathing, while others had eyes which were only just barely closed, as though they were pretending, waiting for the night when they would crawl off and continue to live at the expense of Piyusya and the other proletarians. Then Chepurny and Piyusya decided to give the bourgeoisie supplementary insurance against any continuation of their lives. They reloaded their revolvers and in strict sequence gave each reclining man of property a shot sideways through the throat, in the region of the glands. 'Now our task will be a little more dead certain', Chepurny sighed, the business finally done. 'There's no proletarian on earth that's poorer than a dead man.' . . .

---

23 Andrei Platonov, 'Yuvenil'noe more' [The juvenile sea], in *Efirnyi trakt*, 378.
24 Platonov, *Chevengur*, 184.

The Chekists finished up towards first light, then chucked all the corpses into the pit, along with their bundles. The wives of the murdered men did not dare come close, so they waited for the end of the earthwork from afar. When the Chekists had scattered the left-over dirt on the dawn-lit, empty square so that there would be no dirt for a grave mound, had stuck their spades in the ground and lit up their cigarettes, then the wives of the dead began to advance towards them from all the streets of Chevengur.[25]

We can see in these excerpts how the boundary between the exterior and the interior vibrates (in any case, for us), but the eunuch of the soul does not notice it: he is everywhere, his gaze penetrates the dead Bozhev, we hear the crunch of cervical vertebrae, we even see how time speeds up, as if with the help of *Zeitlupe* [slow motion], the bullet that hit the human body 'grows over with fat'. An optics of a mass murder. This is the source of the entire magic of Platonov's language that suffers from a rupture between the literalness of the image of the event and its meaning: the transmission of the physical event, reduced to the work of random forces, creates alienation from what is being read, for we are not eunuchs of the soul and we do know (even if we know only later, as if caught by surprise) that we are not faced with the ordinary mechanics of the collision of physical bodies ('flesh' meeting 'lead'), but with people being murdered. However, a sudden realisation regarding what is going on cannot be attributed to the emergence of some meaning that restores a lost balance with the world of history ('it happened that way', 'it was a mistake', 'savagery', 'fanaticism', 'a crime against humanity' and so on). When we read *Chevengur*, the realm of senselessness of what takes place will only grow, and it will not give us a chance to take a position of compassion or judgement. We must accept everything as it is or stop reading completely. We must experience on our own skin how inexorably moves the boundary between the interior and the exterior, between what we can master as meaning and what denies meaning. It is a different world, a different space, a different time, perhaps it is much closer to us than the rational constructions with which we relentlessly project the exterior, wishing to find a world free from the madness of Platonov's characters.

---

25   Ibid., 185–6.

The depictions of the *exterior* also reveal the experience of sexuality in Platonov's world. The sexual act is portrayed as an instantaneous flash of a deathly feeling, its 'experience' is objective: an orgasm is an example of physiological transformation; it is the result of a spontaneous and random displacement of internal organs. The regulator of the act is the 'heart'. It would be naive to deny the failure of the heart muscle, as the heart itself here is not so much an image as a witness to the author's asceticism (his 'struggle against'). Only the individual heroes of *Chevengur* and *The Foundation Pit* experience something like a sexual appetite, while others, lacking gender – and this is the overwhelming number of characters – are seen as revolutionary ascetics. It is understandable then that a spontaneous expression of sexual sentiment (for example, masturbation) is interpreted not only as a defeat vis-à-vis biological necessity, but also as a sign of doubt of the revolutionary cause. So, it seems that not all actions are surrendered to the revolution, it seems there are still questions – does this mean that the revolution is not one's main preoccupation? The revolution for Dvanov, the hero of *Chevengur*, is an event after which life ceases to have time; in the revolution one finds another time, a time that does not belong to the revolutionaries. Therefore, sexual love is possible only during instants of life that are already beyond the revolutionary period.

> Dvanov himself felt neither joy nor total oblivion. The entire while he listened attentively to the precise higher wailings of his heart. Then however the heart gave up, slowed, knocked a bit, and slammed shut, but it was already empty. It had opened too wide and accidentally released its single bird.[26]

> He grabbed the horse's leg with both hands, and the leg was transformed into the fragrant living body of that woman whom he did not yet know and would not recognise, but who became mysteriously vital to him now. Dvanov had understood the mystery of hair. His heart rose into his throat and he screamed in the oblivion of his liberation and immediately he sensed an unburdening, satisfied calm. Nature did not neglect to take from Dvanov that for which he had been born into the delirium of his mother, the seed of propagation, which would form

---

26   Ibid., 90.

of new people a family. Life's last minutes flowed on and Sonya pre-
vailed deeply upon Dvanov's hallucinations.[27]

Simon embraced her glumly, then lifted her from the hard stone to the
soft mound of his mother's grave, his feet in the lower grass. He forgot
whether there were still other people in the cemetery or if they had all
left. Sofia Alexandrovna turned away from him in the lumps of that
earth, which held the fine dust of the graves of others, brought up from
the depths by spades.[28]

We notice that an orgasm is not preceded by a desire to possess any
particular woman; there is no love, rather an orgasm is only a memory
of desire, a realisation that once there was also ordinary earthly love.
Although we have to add another statement, perhaps the most important thing, and that is what Platonov himself unwittingly points out: an
orgasm is an instantaneous form of an exchange of energy of life between
kindred bodies under the sign of the growing sense of death; it is this
sense that stimulates desire. And death is the punishment for incest,
because Platonov's characters are indeed brothers and sisters.

Language Executioner

Piyusya went into houses at random, picking out the most adult bourgeois there and silently socking him in the head. Then he said, 'You
read the order?' 'I read it, comrade', the bourgeois answered calmly.
'Just check my documents. I'm not bourgeois, I'm a former Soviet civil
servant and I am liable to be called back into the civil service at the
first necessity.'[29]

One can, of course, assume that Platonov tried to give a literary form
to a non-literary language: various local peasant and city dialects, the
jargon of technocratic utopias, the 'class-revolutionary' rhetoric of the
turbulent times. In other words, it is tempting to see only a certain

---

27   Ibid., 72.
28   Ibid., 301.
29   Ibid., 202.

stylisation in Platonov's language. But what if we assume that his language is put together in a completely different manner?[30] This language is not composed of different dialects (which is the requirement for a socially stratified and established literary language); it has nothing to do with the linguistic inventions of writers like Alexei Remizov or Nikolai Leskov. This language can be called *als ob* language ('as-if' language). The expression *als ob* is not a sign of stylisation, it contains no traces of the author's position in relation to the linguistic material. I use the idea of *als ob* language as the main modality of Platonov's writing in order to point to the hidden non-linguistic force that makes Platonov's language the way it is. It is the force of a *cosmocratic utopia* that acts within and against the spoken language. Platonov's language emerges as a phenomenon of meaning where everyday language is deformed by foreign destructive forces: the everyday word no longer corresponds to the sacred word in the order of descending meaning. On the contrary, now the communal speech behaviour acquires the qualities of sacred speech. The ability to take over everyday vocabulary is connected with the purity of a utopian view. Platonov's language is the outcome of the war of languages: the war between *cosmocratic* (cosmic or universal) language and the language of people, a *secular*, or *secularised* language.[31] We cannot escape the anxious

---

30   The revolutionary epoch always tries to rename everything. Even when the revolutionary dialect of the peasant class corresponds to the truth of the linguistic fact, for a literature of the revolutionary time such language should not exist; a new language is being created, it is not borrowed from anywhere. Velemir Khlebnikov was trying to develop a universal, 'cosmic' language of the Revolution, to create the most authentic linguistic machine for producing new meanings.

31   Platonov's language is event-based, and not every literary language has this ability. Some languages are informational, that is, they simply report what happened, for example, during the years of Stalin's purges. Other languages are coloured with their authors' personal story, with the suffering they underwent (memories, diaries, documentary prose). Among historical studies there are absolutely unique works, such as Solzhenitsyn's *Gulag Archipelago* that combines two linguistic layers (biographical and historical-documentary) on the basis of a single language of denunciation, a sort of meta-language. Something similar can be found in Alexander Zinoviev, though with a stronger emphasis on denunciation of the 'Soviet system'; his novels turn into sociological-satirical-logical studies. In any case, the *meta-language* is an extratemporal interpretation of an event for which there is no adequate language; or the author simply does not need such a language; or, on the contrary, he thinks that such a language is impossible. The meta-language is controlled from the high position of time of those who are not dependent on the event, who survived, who won. It can be said that Solzhenitsyn's and Zinoviev's 'novels-histories', and even Shalamov's sincere true stories, choose their literary meta-language in order not to simply report about the event, but to make the

feeling that all these strange images, figures and bodies that come before us are somehow close to us. By mixing together directives, slogans, instructions and orders with the improbability of the communist utopias, the language of the victorious class penetrated the everyday speech, and today we find it increasingly difficult to understand this speech, even though Platonov's literature speaks a language that is part of our own heritage as post-Soviet cultural readers.

After a few minutes of reading Platonov's *The Foundation Pit*, we discover the wonderful power of his language, which takes away our usual trust in reality and pushes us in a different direction, toward the truth. Now we understand our own artificiality as living beings; we discover that we are the substrates of language and nothing more. The tragic comedy of a Platonov character is that he is sentenced to death by language. This means that anyone who tries to master the language of the *impossible* (the utopian) and speak it as a language of everyday life is condemned to death. This sentence should not be taken as a metaphor. The sentence of death in this case has a literal meaning: such language does sentence to death all who attempt to speak it. And, by virtue of its terrorist might, it is capable of threatening other languages and dialects, other bodies, earthly or heavenly, and other spaces where there is still speech that is not subjugated by the language-executioner. As the cosmocratic language begins to unfold, all natural-organic, spontaneously formed connections between human beings are destroyed. Each body-character dies with every word it utters. This language wants to 'come true' whatever it takes, even though there will be no one left to speak it. The cosmocratic word negates its own meaning in action.[32]

---

readers trust the author who is located both inside and outside the described events (and who is therefore able to tell us about these events).

32   Cf. 'It is not difficult to see, that since we use slogans and expressions in our socio-political everyday lives that lost their meaning and their purpose, our thinking as well becomes meaningless. One can think in images, one can think in terms, but can one think in linguistic exemplars that, despite being clichés, continue to claim to have expressive and influential power? This kind of thinking can, in fact, only be "meaningless". By taking a particular turn of speech or a linguistic formula to be a living slogan, we take a simple name of thought as its content. By using this or that traditional expression, or by using fossilised phraseology, and by continuing to see in them specific stylistic purpose, we cease to understand what we are saying. We do not know what "the advance of capital" really means when we use that phrase for a hundredth or a thousandth time . . .' (Grigorii Vinokour, *Kultura iazyka* [The culture of language], Moscow, 2006, 121).

What is a *revolutionary* language?[33] For Platonov, it is the language of the semi-literate peasant masses, who have gained access to the revolutionary consciousness of the future. A revolutionary, or cosmocratic, language passes through two stages before becoming the language of the masses: a transformative stage and a bureaucratic stage. The first represents and describes the work of *human-machines*; the second deals with orders and slogans, directives and decisions, i.e. the entire abundant new language of post-revolutionary bureaucracy.[34] The ordinary language, immersed in the language of pseudo-revolutionary slogans, creates a

---

33   Here is an excellent example of the transformation of the French language during the period of the French Revolution: 'Speaking and writing without concern for tradition, they [the revolutionaries] left the narrow circle that imprisoned polite language; without realising it and without meaning to do so, they destroyed in no time the work of Hôtel de Rambouillet and the epoch of Louis XIV. Without any embarrassment they used familiar words and expressions whose strength and usefulness they had learned from daily use, not worrying that they would be banished from the Court and the salons. They used provincialisms from their places of origin; they used the terms of their trades and businesses, forged the words they lacked and changed the meaning of those that no longer suited them. The Revolution was truly a creator in the realm of language, as well as in the realm of political institutions' (Paul Lafargue, 'La langue française avant et après la Révolution', in *Critiques littéraires*, Paris: Editions Sociales Internationales, 1936, 55 [35–86]).

34   Platonov's language is similar to argot (i.e. something that is untranslatable into normative language). It is a mixed language, where we see coexistence of a language of the cosmocratic and the revolutionary, and of an everyday speech of the peasant masses of the time; we can also add here the influence of urban speech and of literary examples. 'I think it is more accurate to treat argot as a double language, where the argotic series is taken as the primary and the original, while the second language series is something that must be found (rather than simply claiming that the literary language is something primary)' (Boris Larin, *Istoriya russkogo iazyka i obshchee iazykoznanie* [The history of the Russian language and general linguistics], Moscow, 1977, 185). This inversion of the language, the tectonic shift of the lower linguistic strata to the top, reflects the development of the revolution's social ideas. The Bolshevik-communist everyday jargon became the only language that was undermining the traditional cultural norms of the literary language. Almost all the leading writers of the time (Zoshchenko, Babel, Pilnyak, Ilf and Petrov, Zamyatin) took part in the language war against the former 'bourgeois' construction of the world. But perhaps only Platonov endowed this language war with such ruthless poetic meaning. In essence, he created a literary 'ideo-lect' that reflected the experience of the revolutionary self-consciousness of the masses. The revolutionary slogans, which invaded the pre-linguistic elements of the popular dialects, created a special linguistic – cosmocratic – consciousness. The order coming to the masses from the revolutionary centre of power names the world anew, i.e. it immediately rebuilds it, and it cannot otherwise be. When we read Platonov, we seem to be present at the moment of the revolutionary rebuilding of the common everyday ('bourgeois') language. This new language-executioner infiltrated everything and became everything: things,

comic effect, even though it is in fact a language of the all-encompassing social violence.

Here are the examples of slogans, announcements, orders and instructions mentioned by Platonov in some of his novels and stories:

'Sovietisation as the Beginning of Harmonisation'[35]

'Every day we live through is a nail in the head of the bourgeoisie, so let us live forever, its head can suffer for it!'[36]

'On the coordination of workers within the sub-department assigned to me, with a view to the rationalisation of the agricultural enterprises of the province commanded by me . . .'[37]

'R.S.F.S.R. Main warehouses of bone processing and cotton paper industry of the regional scale. As depicted by painter Pupkov.'[38]

'Proletarian prophet Elijah: The Leningrad Soviet scientist, Professor Martensen, has invented airplanes which will spontaneously disperse rain on the land and will create clouds above the farmland. During the coming summer it has been proposed to test these airplanes in peasant surroundings. The airplanes do all this by means of iodised sand.'[39]

An order (a directive) – *a slogan* (of the day) – *a poster* (agitation), this is the sequence of actions introducing a political decision to the masses. Yuri Tynyanov analysed the 'new language' [*novoyaz*] of the Russian Revolution in more precise linguistic terms. For him, the slogan is 'a word whose lexical unity is limited to one connection, and its basic sign is attached to a particular thing.'[40] For example, the revolutionary slogan 'Expropriate the expropriators!' is clearly inferior to the Russian equivalent 'Rob what was robbed (rob the robbers)' because it is limited in its connections with what it signifies; the Russian phrase has more

people, missiles, weapons, pain and suffering; it is as new as the language of the biblical Adam who named things for the first time.

35 Andrei Platonov, 'The City of Gradov', trans. Friederike Snyder, in *Collected Works*, Ann Arbor: Ardis, 1978, 404.

36 Andrei Platonov, 'Sokrovennyi chelovek' ['The innermost man'], in *Efirnyi trakt*, 173.

37 Platonov, 'The City of Gradov', 398.

38 Andrei Platonov, 'Buchilo' ['The sink-hole'], in *Usomnivshyisya Makar. Rasskazy 1920kh godov. Stikhotvoreniya*, 62.

39 Platonov, 'The City of Gradov', 400.

40 Yuri Tynyanov, *Problema stikhotvornogo iazyka. Stati'i* [The problem of poetic language. Essays], Moscow, 1963, 210.

possibilities for being understood by an audience, even if this audience is new to the context of the slogan; the Russian version is dynamic and effective as a slogan. The revolutionary or *cosmocratic* language sought to become the original condition for the *direct* influence of the government on the masses. Phrases-slogans, orders or directives, instructions and ordinances are political performatives. The phrase-slogan points to the only decision regarding the necessary action for all without exception: it is directed at an individual as a representative of the masses. There is a grammatical equality of all statements (one and the same phrase structure). It can be said that in this communist kingdom there are only dead people, or psycho-machines like them, who cannot properly execute the programme of life. Hence, we see the tragicomic nature of practically all of Platonov's heroes when their language touches the ground, tools, human bodies and machines (I mean, of course, Platonov's anti-utopian novels).

The cosmocratic or revolutionary language is made up of slogans. Each slogan has a dual structure: on the one hand, a demonstration of its strength (announcements, instructions, posters, orders), and on the other, a plan of specific actions that must be followed. Platonov's characters are different in terms of their occupations, feelings, positions and fates, but they are all located within the zone of action of the original Order, the order-toward-death, which they execute as if they are 'dead'. But what is the nature of this order? Here is the answer: 'It is the secret of the genuine language of command that it does not make promises but imposes demands. The deepest fortune of men consists in being sacrificed, and the highest art of command consists in showing purposes worthy of this sacrifice.'[41] After all, an order is something that

---

41   Ernst Jünger, *The Worker: Dominion and Will*, trans. Bogdan Costea and Laurence Paul Hemming, Evanston, IL: Northwestern University Press, 2017, 49. As Elias Canetti puts it: 'A command addressed to a large number of people thus has a very special character. It is intended to make a crowd of them and, in as far as it succeeds in this, it does not arouse fear. The slogan of a demagogue, impelling people in a certain direction, has exactly the same function; it can be regarded as a command addressed to large numbers. From the point of view of the crowd, which wants to come into existence quickly and to maintain itself as a unit, such slogans are useful and indeed indispensable. The art of a speaker consists in compressing all his aims into slogans. By hammering them home he then engenders a crowd and helps to keep it in existence. He creates the crowd and keeps it alive by a comprehensive command from above. Once he has achieved this, it scarcely matters what he demands. A speaker can insult and threaten an assemblage of people in

does not have an equivalent in any other form of utterance: it is singular, unique and directed at addressing a particular task. An order that is not executed is a nonsensical notion. An order has ancient guarantees of obligatory execution – death (now replaced by an oath). Often an order is an institution of class domination. True, there are different sorts of orders: one kind of order is directed at *one* person, another kind at *many* people. In the first case, it is about reworking the order, its depth of immersion into the memory of the individual, about what Canetti calls the *sting* of the order. In Platonov, an individual order takes precedence over an order directed at everyone. Platonov does not deal with the masses, their movements and impulses (as opposed to Vertov or Eisenstein). In Platonov each character hears an order individually, which is why his consciousness splits in two: he is ready to execute the order, but in the execution itself he manages to find freedom for *escape* and withdrawal, i.e. for his individual life. An individual choice and a revolutionary order do not match, but, in Platonov's world, one does not exist without the other.

One important element in Platonov's tactic is the use of personal names. In essence, naming pushes out the use of personal pronouns (if they are used at all, it is often only as support for the name). What does this lead to? To the situation where each phrase is perceived separately from any other phrase, where it receives a distinct performativity, i.e. it becomes an event of action. Of course, we can also recall the so-called revolutionary address: *comrade Ivanov*. One is addressed not by name and patronymic, but by surname. And that is a very revealing operation of sublation of all personal relationships. Platonov's method consists precisely in creating a contrast between the impersonal address by surname and the existing relationships of attraction, sympathy, participation, assistance and love that arise between his heroes. For example, in *Chevengur*, in around three pages of text, the hero called Serbinov is mentioned more than thirty times by his surname (which is almost never replaced with 'he' or 'his'). Although his name is singled out, it is not an individual name; it does not represent a person but a type. The proper name turns into an outpost of a grammatically primitive phrase.

the most terrible way and they will still love him if, by doing so, he succeeds in forming them into a crowd' (Elias Canetti, *Crowds and Power*, trans. Carol Stewart, New York: Continuum, 1984, 311).

In everyday grammar, names are deprived of their individual aura. But, conversely, a number of other names are endowed with individuality, names that are now separated by clear terminological boundaries: *Collectivisation, Revolution, Industrialisation (steam locomotive), Communism, Substance, Existence*. During the first years of Soviet industrialisation, the Bolsheviks managed to rename childhood: 'At the North Pole there was a pillar of white flame burning in the sky and commemorating the electrification of the world. Little girls were given names such as Electrification, Spark, Wave, Energy, Dynamic Machine, Atmosphere, Mystery. And the boys were called Bolt, Electron, Cylinder, Sheave, Discharge, Ampere, Current, Degree, Micron.'[42]

Indeed, our presence in the world is established not because we see or feel, but because we hear our own voice, a voice that we distinguish from the choir of many other voices. We have a unique and inimitable voice. It is precisely 'my voice' that is trying, to the extent that other voices allow it, to achieve a state of maximal closeness to itself and to the world. My *presence-in-the-world* is the original closeness that my voice gives me: the world must repeat what I say, accept my voice as a shell that absorbs and preserves the noises of the sea; even my whisper must be heard, even my silence. The voice is the sound contour of my body; I touch the world with it, and the world touches me by means of it. But Platonov's world is not my world; it lacks precisely this internal human voice. And it cannot be there since Platonov's language is *performative*: its task is not to represent physical actions and events, but *to perform* them. In other words, the action itself appears as a kind of simulation of the 'work' of language and does not stand on its own. Each articulated type of body acquires a specific nomenclature of linguistic acts. More precisely: the subject of the action is the language, not the body of this or that character. The language of slogans/orders creates bodies: Zhachev (the body of a pseudo-cripple), Chiklin (the ideal body of labour and terror), Voshchev (the body of exhaustion, perverse body), Dvanov (the body of revolutionary ascesis and intellectualism). The nomenclature of corporeal images is fluid and fragile. All instances of self-naming, self-dressing, exposure of the bodies of the characters, act as linguistic performative acts. The goal is to create new bodies using words alone:

---

42   Andrei Platonov, 'Zhazhda nishchego' [The thirst of the poor], in *Sochinenia, Tom pervyi, 1918–1927, Kniga pervaya*, 167–8.

Ignatii Pashentsev takes the name of *Fyodor Dostoevsky*, one can also put on a knight's armour, as does another character in *Chevengur*, or one can fuse with the body of Rosa Luxemburg, the *motherly body* of the revolution (as does Kopenkin), or with the body of the *father*, as does Dvanov. The language names and connects, transforms and erases, carries out a continuous transformation of the characters' bodies by virtue of its dominance over a concrete physical action. No corporeal event is possible without language.

An instant of decision: on the one hand, we have a performative language of the cosmocratic utopia (*tragedy*), a language that contains in itself certain utterances-actions and therefore is a language that produces reality, body and space itself; on the other hand, we cannot completely reject the need to look for safe distances and all the pleasures of life that these distances provide us with when we detach ourselves, elude or escape to save ourselves, and here laughter occupies its rightful place (*comedy*). Language as *per-formation* and language as *performance*. Language that instantly transforms utterances into actions; language as an action independent of any teleology; action as a pure act of desire. This is how two series of events (a comic one and a tragic one) are revealed (not without the help of the *eunuch of the soul*); they move in parallel, and yet as though through one another. By asserting its infinite might in acts of performance, the cosmocratic body enters the sphere of self-destruction, but we, the readers, refuse to follow its example.[43]

---

43   At first, the criticism of Platonov's work was 'perceptive' to his style and aesthetics; it was thorough, but not bloodthirsty. 'All of Platonov's people are dead. Therefore, a final physical death does not frighten them. The transition from indifference to non-being. Where's the line? Where's the transition? The only difference is that final non-being has not yet been experienced, so it is unknown. It is mysterious, and therefore, even a person exhausted by despair and hopelessness is curious about it and is drawn to it. Suicide, death, for such a person is the last hope for another, special, actual life' (Abram Gurvich, 'Andrei Platonov', in *Andrei Platonov. Vospominaniya sovremennikov* [Andrei Platonov. Recollections of contemporaries], Moscow, 1994, 365). And here is how Platonov acknowledged his 'errors': 'In my works, people move as if they were killed by capitalism. It all happened because the bourgeoisie, on the eve of the revolution, brought some workers to such a state that the most vital element – the revolutionary consciousness – had been taken out of them. However, the reality is the opposite. It is clear that by portraying workers as dead figures that move spontaneously, I have made the sharpest perversion of reality that one could think of, that one could work out' (ibid., 296). Platonov's vision, as we know, cannot be otherwise, and no matter how many justifications he provided, he can see the world only this way.

'Letters to the Leader' as a Genre

A fierce argument exists precisely regarding Platonov's style. In essence, all criticism, starting with Stalin's comments on the margins of the manuscript of *Vprok* [For future use] ('What a bastard!', 'Scoundrel!' and so on), accurately focuses attention on his 'little words', phrases, agrammatisms, accusing Platonov of appearing as a fully self-conscious secular 'holy fool'. But the point is not that Platonov is an oddball writer who writes about whatever comes to his mind; things are much more serious (especially from the point of view of the despotic Stalin and his literary servants). Everything that is the natural essence of Platonov's style is rejected as a direct mockery of the Soviet reality. Platonov defends himself and says he is not a satirist and that he considers himself a *political writer*, thinking that this would free him of the charge of disloyalty to the regime: 'I did not consider myself a satirist, nor did I try to be a satirist. I was looking for opportunities to be a political writer.'[44] Wittingly or unwittingly, Platonov participated in the class war (in the village). It is clear that he created his incredible images (imitations of popular dialects, archaisms, various 'little words', sayings and proverbs) not only so that he could depict something real. Although we must admit that this artificial, invented language was the only method of representing a silent popular consciousness. The critics (following Stalin's lead) pointed out the 'mocking' style of Platonov's playing at politics; they did not regard it as related to a particular literary genre but saw it as a conscious ridiculing of the values of socialism. And this was not simply a question of style. It was something more serious: what language should we use to speak about the 'Revolution' (and using which genres)? Platonov chooses a proverb-like approach, which means that he very consciously aims to avoid realistic details and simple storytelling techniques. Everything is given in minimal proportions, everything is shortened, I would even say, super-condensed; the goal is to use something extremely small in order to express something extremely large. This is the entire strength of Platonov's style. As soon as you turn your attention away from the pre-Gulag reality of socialist construction (*tragedy*), you begin to feel the revolutionary meaninglessness of the ordinary human effort (*comedy*).

---

44 'Stenogramma tvorcheskogo vechera Andreya Platonova' [A transcript of a meeting dedicated to the work of Andrei Platonov], in *Andrei Platonov. Vospominaniya sovremennikov*, 300.

The Despot, through a set of repressive measures (a technology of terror), has created his own discourse, which exists alongside literature as its unreachable exemplar. Although, in reality, literature exists inside this discourse; moreover, it sets its rhythm and provides it with rules. The despotic discourse is the discourse of reality; it is orientated in accordance with an order (where disobedience means death). He who does not obey the Despot can be easily eliminated. In other words, it is a pattern of political behaviour that everyone should emulate (with an emphasis on diligence rather than 'accuracy' of emulation). There is no accounting for tastes, but the Despot's tastes must be accounted for. It is impossible to predict how he will act and what decisions he will make. There is only one hope that remains – to forestall his possible decision with a personal letter.

Here is Platonov's letter to Stalin:

Comrade Stalin,

I am requesting your attention even though I have not yet earned it with my actions. In order to not waste your time, I will be brief, perhaps to the detriment of the clarity of the matter. My novel *Vprok* appeared in the journal *Krasnaya Nov'*. It was written over a year ago. The comrades from RAPW [Russian Association of Proletarian Writers] leadership thought this work to be extremely harmful from the ideological point of view. Having reread my novel, I changed my mind about many things; I noticed in it things that were not visible to me when I was writing it, but that were obvious to any proletarian person: it contained the spirit of kulaks, the spirit of irony, as well as ambiguities, deceptions, false stylistics, etc. It turned out to be a harmful work indeed, for it could only be interpreted to mean to cause harm to the collective farm movement. But the collective farm movement is the most precious, the most, so to speak, 'difficult' product of the revolution. This product, like a child, requires enormous, close attention, even as one approaches it. But I, to put it briefly, produced some sort of counter-revolutionary propaganda (the author's original intention does not change the situation, the result is what matters most). I write this to you quite directly, even though I am still saddened by this situation.

I realised that the comrades from RAPW were correct that I lost my way and that I am about to perish. Last year, in the summer, I visited some collective farms in the middle Volga region (after I finished *Vprok*). There, I saw and felt what the socialist reorganisation of the village really meant, what the collective farms meant for the poor and the hired hands, for all working peasants. There, I saw the collective farm people who astonished my consciousness, and there I also had the chance to see the kulaks and those who helped them. The concrete facts were so profound, and at times tragic in their content, that my soul coagulated; I understood what terrible, dark forces were standing up against the world of socialism, and what immense work was needed from everyone whose hope was in socialism. As a result of the trip, as a result of the ideological assistance of a number of great comrades, the real Bolsheviks, I have rejected my earlier works internally and artistically, but I also had to reject them politically, they had to be destroyed and no longer published. That was my error, my weakness of understanding of the situation. Then I started to work on a new book, testing myself, catching myself at every phrase and every proposition; agonisingly and slowly, I was overcoming the inertia of lies and vulgarity that still owned me, and which was hostile to the proletariat and the collective farm workers. As a result of my work and my new, proletarian, approach to reality, things felt easier and lighter as if I was returning home from faraway places.

Now the criticism of RAPW has explained to me that *Vprok* is a harmful work for the collective farms and for the political position that serves as a hope for all working peasants around the world. Knowing that you are at the head of this political position, that in it, in the political position of the Party, is found the care of millions, I am setting aside all care for my own person and will attempt to find a way to reduce the harm caused by the publication of the novel *Vprok*. I will do so by writing and publishing a work that will bring ideological and artistic benefit to the proletarian reader ten times more than the harm of the demoralising counter-revolutionary irony that was objectively contained in *Vprok*.

All I care about now is to reduce the damage caused by my past literary activity. I have been working on this since last autumn, but now I have to make a tenfold effort, because the only way out is to create a work that will atone for the damage caused by *Vprok*. In addition to this main undertaking, I will also issue a statement in the press acknowledging the harmful errors of my literary work; and I will do it in such a way as to make others afraid of doing the same, so that it is clear that any literary output that objectively harms the proletariat is treachery, and that this treachery is especially egregious when it is per- petrated by a proletarian man. It is clear that such a statement would only be a promise to atone for my guilt but not the atonement itself. However, I have never before issued such statements and I would not have done so if I did not know that I would fulfil my promise.

Comrade Stalin, I heard that you appreciate literature and are interested in it. If you have read or will ever read *Vprok*, then you are likely, as I now know, to severely condemn this delusional work, because you are the leader of the socialist reorganisation of the village, and so this matter is closer to your heart than it is to any other person. With this letter, I do not hope to diminish the vile nature of *Vprok* but I want you to know how the case is seen by the one who is responsible for this text, its author, and what he is doing to liquidate the errors of his ways.

After rereading this letter to you, I wanted to add something that would serve as a clear expression of my actual attitude toward the socialist construction. But I will have the right to do so only when I will have become useful for the revolution.

Respectfully yours,

Andrei Platonov, 8 June 1931[45]

---

45   *Novaya Gazeta* 8:531 (1–7 March 1999), publication prepared by Tamara Dubin- skaya and Timur Dzhalilov. Here is what the editors say about the letter: 'We publish here the letter to Stalin by one of Russia's most talented writers, Andrei Platonov (1899–1951); it was written shortly after the publication of his novel *Vprok. Bedniatskaia khronika* [For future use. A poor peasant's chronicle] in *Krasnaya Nov'* [Virgin red soil] (1931, No. 3). According to the memoirs of Platonov's contemporaries, Vyacheslav Polonsky and Vladimir Sutyrin, Stalin called the novel "kulak-sympathising and vile". Already in the fifth and the sixth issues of *Krasnaya Nov'*, *Vprok* was sharply criticised by Alexan- der Fadeev in an article called "Ob odnoi bedniatskoi khronike" [On one poor peasant's chronicle], which included a final note: "From the editorial board: the editorial board joins Fadeev's assessment of Platonov's novel and thinks that it was a gross mistake to have it printed in *Krasnaya Nov'*." At the plenary session of RAPW on 4 June 1931, Platonov was declared to be an 'agent of the bourgeoisie and the kulaks in literature' (*Na literaturnom postu* [On the literary guard], 1931, No. 21–2). Many articles about the 'extremely harmful' novel *Vprok* appeared after Andrei Platonov's letter to Stalin. A typed version of the letter was sent to Gorky by I.P. Tovstukha, Stalin's closest assistant (who had worked in his secretariat since December of 1921). The copy was kept in the Archive of the President of the Russian Federation, and in the early 1990s transferred to

The letter of repentance became a necessary condition for correlating the literary experience and its political template. First and foremost, one had to reject literature as a personal undertaking, for it is precisely this rejection that is seen in the recognition of one's political errors and the condemnation of oneself for one's 'incorrect', non-proletarian understanding of the aims of literature. When the template is identified, acknowledged and evaluated, the author's repentance becomes appropriate. One cannot say that Platonov and many other Soviet cultural figures (of those working in the genre of 'letters to the Leader') were not sincere, even though their sincerity was politically motivated.[46] How does the Despot gain a moral advantage over his victims? By very simple means: he creates a special encouraging environment – an environment of denunciation. Everyone denounces everyone else, and the main object of denunciation is the artist himself (even if the artist is often given many signs of admiration by the Despot, it does not mean he will manage to stay alive). A letter of repentance is a counterpart of a denunciation, or, more precisely, it is an attempt to forestall such a denunciation, to weaken it.

Platonov desperately attempted to redo his novels this way or that way, but only a fool would take this desperation to be the sign of his reformation; he still remained under suspicion as he was not able to give up his own peculiar manner of writing. What we see then is the marginalisation of a literary experience and, in essence, a civil execution of the artist. In a proverb, unlike in any other type of narrative, everything can be interpreted. Thus, Platonov invented a language that all of his heroes spoke, pretending that he merely described and reported, i.e. that he was guided only by the truth of observation. That was already a challenge to the Despot's power. At the level of family, friendship and love, creative work and rest, travels, in all the collectives that a person encountered in Stalin's era, there existed the same implicit split that was ready to reveal the abyss that the Despot tried to create between people. The discourse of despotic power, unlimited and absolutely illegitimate, was pervasive.

the Archive of the Gorky Institute of World Literature. The printed version is based on that copy (archival reference PTL 12–113–1).

46   Many wrote these letters to the leader, for example: Sergei Eisenstein, Mikhail Bulgakov, Mikhail Zoshchenko, Ilya Erenburg, Kornei Chukovsky, Evgeni Zamyatin and others. They wrote in different ways, but still only for one purpose: to exonerate themselves, to try to save their work and their family.

Stalin-the-despot was an intermediate link; he was the link between words and things; he imposed on society the experience of the Soviet labour camp; and yet he himself also depended on this experience.

Platonov's language is a remarkable example of a *negative mimesis* of the oppressive language-executioner, created by the might of an autocratic and unlimited will. Only one rule remains: to imitate by negating the imitated.

2

History as Nature

'The main thing is to think up some kind of figure.' Dvanov drew a figure on a sheet of paper. He gave the sketch to the president and explained. 'The eight on its side signifies eternity of time and the upright arrow with two heads means infinity of space.'[1]

Emptying Out: Figures and Bodies

Platonov – the inventor of machines, the ameliorator and the geopolitician – possessed an amazing ability to sense space. It is sufficient to recall the great space that moves in our direction from the pages of *The Juvenile Sea*, *Chevengur* or *The Foundation Pit*. Platonov's world is surrounded by this active space, by the emptiness of the steppe landscape, captured by the yearning of abandoned villages, dry riverbeds, black wounds of ravines . . . There's no place in this world where one can rest, lie down, take shelter. In this world one can only move aimlessly without stopping; and that is the only way to get comfortable in this space. The purpose of this space is to empty out, erase and disperse. This space must be empty . . . Uninhabited space is dangerous. For Platonov, space is more than what one could appreciate in terms of our terrestrial points of reference and similarities. And it's not even space as such that matters here, but

---

1   Platonov, *Chevengur*, 108.

a continuous act of emptying out. Therefore, to be able to discern this space is to sense, along with Platonov, the increasing degree of the Earth's desolation. Space is what limits itself, what is external to itself. Even those spaces that we only conditionally designate as such, for example, dream spaces or literary spaces, have *their own* minimum of spatiality. We should also note that Platonov uses the term 'space' differently; more often than not, it designates a state rather than a limit or something that includes something else in itself. The state of space indicates cancellation or instability of limits, their possible limit-ation. The state is that which takes place, not that which is or has been. What happens is what we call *emptying out* of space. Properly speaking, words like *pustosh* [emptiness], *pustynya* [desert], *pustyr'* [wasteland] open an extremely rich sequence of prefixes based on the verb *pustit'/ne pustit'* [to (not) allow, to (not) let in] – to allow/forbid us to access a certain 'place'. But the main thing here is the possibility of free action that assumes that there is no longer any space that stretches out or is filled up; there is only space that is emptied out, becomes uninhabitable, unsettled, disintegrated and deadened. There is no more space to interfere with a grandiose machinic reorganisation of nature. But this is only one aspect of the 'empty' and the 'emptied out'. After all, one should not forget that Platonov's heroes are desert-dwellers and wanderers who refuse to embrace the new world; one should not forget their escapism and their burdensome necrophilia that resembles the 'Russian longing'.[2]

Let us take a look at how Platonov sees this 'space':

The expanses of plains and fields lay in emptiness and silence, exhaling vapors like new-mown hay, while the late sun toiled alone in the slumbering heights above Chevengur.[3]

The moonlight timidly illuminated the steppe, and all about the expanses presented themselves to the eye as though they already lay in the next world, where life is contemplative, pale, and unfeeling, where in the glimmering silence a man's shadow rustles in the grass. Several people left communism for the depths of the advancing night

---

2   Cf. 'A system of interdependent moving mirrors reflecting the emptiness of one another – this is the terrible objective mechanism of co-innermost-ness all the way to the bottom of the void' (Platonov, *Zapisnye knizhki*, 241).

3   Platonov, *Chevengur*, 258.

and obscurity. Some went to seek wives for themselves and would then return to Chevengur, while others had grown thin on the vegetable fare of Chevengur and went off to other places to eat meat, and one of those who left, only a boy in age, wanted to find his parents no matter where in the world they might be, so he too left.[4]

Above them, as though in the next world, the moon was drawn immaterially along, and was dipping already towards moonset. Its existence was in vain, for the moon did not make plants grow and man slept beneath it silently. The sunlight which lit earth's sister of the night from afar had within it a churning, burning, living substance, but this light reached the moon already filtered through the dead length of space, so that everything churning and alive scattered from it along the way, so all that remained was the true dead light.[5]

The drama of Platonov's writing: an experience of empty and abandoned spaces, an emptying out. It is as if from the very beginning this writing is used to express the longing and boredom of long-distance travel and horizons, to express the beginning of the end of time. The space is captured by the forces that were emptying out the land; it began to grow in emptiness, to disperse bodies, persons, towns and villages, thoughts and feelings. The world is increasingly acquiring non-human qualities, perhaps in order to place itself on a map of a great, soulless land-surveyor who is mapping out the fantastic geometry of the foundation pit.

There are other spaces that are constructed by the multidimensionality of things, events and bodies, that are supported by the power of human time. But Platonov does not sense this sort of space, because he does not sense the permanence of a *thing*, i.e. of everything that fills up and divides, individualises the everyday space. He sees in this space its cracks and flaws; he knows where this space 'leaks' and into what elements it disintegrates. Moreover, he clearly states: 'The thing stood between people and split them into dust. The thing must be destroyed.'[6] The figuration of bodies and their movements is not necessary in Platonov's world (and it is almost entirely absent there), which only confirms our intuition that by space he understands forces that empty out space, that make it empty

---

4   Ibid., 264.
5   Ibid., 267.
6   Platonov, 'Potomki solntsa' [The descendants of the sun], 331.

and impossible to fill up. It is not figures as complexes of bodies-things-events that organise space and divide it in accordance with the measures of distance and proximity, but the force of emptying out, aggressive and impersonal, that moves, dispersing the living, pushing out the richness of multidimensional life toward the dead, the decay of death. That is why the gaze of the eunuch of the soul is so sensitive to the empty qualities of the visible, for behind them there is the original *emptiness* (*Nothing*) that cannot be filled up with human time.

Thus, there are two spaces. One is always filled up and in excess, that is the human space of the things and events closest to us; there are no machines and auxiliary devices here, everything is 'made by hand'. And the other space is that which is being emptied out, the space created by 'science', 'technology' and machines – by these invaders of Nature. It is sufficient to repeat some of Platonov's descriptions of space: *depopulated, submerged in silence, without time, empty, emptied out, extinct, infinite, full of longing and sadness, lunar, homeless, shady, airy, speechless, unknown, motionless, boring, vague, dead, long, scattered, simple.* The observer is linguistically equipped to indicate the presence of this extremely impoverished spatial image:

> Dvanov felt a pang of loss for time which had passed, for time comes ever into being and disappears, while man stays in one place with his hopes for the future, and then Dvanov guessed why Chepurny and the Bolsheviks of Chevengur so wanted communism. Communism is the end of history and the end of time, for time runs only within nature, while within man there stands only melancholy.[7]

The space is a trap in which time is caught and where it dies. The time is almost gone, it crosses over into spatial images, and continues to disintegrate.

The gaze of the 'eunuch of the soul' is a facto-graphic, 'non-blinking' photo-gaze, with iron shutters on the lens; it 'clicks' an image, remembers fragments of what is taking place. The photo-gaze sees the invisible, which creates the background for the emerging figures. Between the characters' figures and their speeches there is the emptiness of a world that has survived an unprecedented social catastrophe. The figure moves against a

---

7   Platonov, *Chevengur*, 273.

depopulated background and is about to stop; the author's voice attempts to explain what is happening, and even to resist the sense of longing and forgetting so characteristic of many of Platonov's heroes. If we look at the figure, the background becomes empty, it empties out; but if we look at the background, we see nothing, or, to be more precise, we consider it in order to extract a new figure from it, with the former figure becoming a contour-limit; we could even say it forms something like a hole until it disappears in the background. Platonov's gaze darts between the figure and the background, erasing their boundaries. Platonov 'writes' figures, not bodies, and for him the figure is what binds the individual bodies and their movements to one curve, the curve of emptying out. The figure is not defined by visible properties, it is a place of transition from one life to another, from visible to invisible, because the figure is not equal to the sum of its constituent elements (bodies); in it all bodies coexist, as in a dream: dead and alive bodies, all events, past and future. Platonov's characters cannot live as individual bodies, but only as part of complex conglomerations, colonies, masses, where a particular body breathes the breath of other bodies and gets energy for life or loses it thanks to a multitude of other bodies. And having moved to this level of existence, where visible and invisible life are indistinguishable, the human body no longer experiences the old fear of emptying out, the end of time, pain and death.

Here is, for example, Kopenkin. A man-warrior-horse, he cannot be separated from his horse named Proletarian Strength, but this bundle of properties is too weak to stay in the field of the visible, and so comes the next series of his transformations as Kopenkin begins to travel along the various steppe roads that are leading him to the grave of Rosa Luxemburg (a mother, a sister and a lover). Kopenkin's army – acting in an unknown jurisdiction, going in unknown directions, participating in unknown battles, defeats and victories – travels along the one and only correct route: a portrait of Rosa is a map that opens the life of the horizon. The figure of Kopenkin is a series of bodies-signs, located at the level of the visible and the invisible life. But there is another series here, a brotherly one: Dvanov – a split, a repetition, a doubling. Platonov does not describe individual bodies, only figures, figurations and configurations of bodies. A figure is a curve that outlines a community of bodies; a single body is assembled from 'parts' of other bodies as soon as it becomes an object of description. The bodies mix and dissolve in a large group; some form symbiotic complexes. A figure is a complex or a plural body that is deployed in motion; it stands against an aggressive background that seeks to blur its boundaries and dissolve them in the desolate spaces of Platonov's landscape. There is no space, only the steppe, and the steppe moves; there is no *place-above-it*, everything in this steppe consists of *places-between-places*. There are no more localities, areas, districts. That is why the scattering of individual bodies and their 'substantial' surroundings, or emptying out, is, for Platonov, a kind of wandering, but wandering in search of one, perhaps impossible figure that would provide an individual with the missing parts of a lost life.[8]

New Death

And new forces, new cadres, may perish before the coming of socialism, but their 'pieces', their sorrow, their flow of emotion will enter the world of the future. Pretty young faces of the Bolsheviks – you will not yet win; your infants will win. The revolution will unfold beyond you! Greetings to all believers and all who are dying from the overload.[9]

An emptiable, empty, uninhabited space – the eunuch of the soul sees this non-human landscape as the universal framework of the world. But does this strange creature also see anything else? Probably not, because it only reacts to the growth of emptiness, gathering it everywhere: from human bodies and figures, voices, from Earth and Cosmos. Platonov's world is so oppressively deserted that invisible life has gained in it the superiority over visible life. Under the influence of the force of the invisible, the visible disintegrates, dissipates. The emptiness grows through death as those who are near and distant, those who are loved and unloved,

---

8 The idea of 'free lands' and 'escape' indeed opened a new space for peasants-serfs, one not under the control of the arbitrary imperial rule and violence. Kirill Chistov pointed out that the conflict between the central government and the peasantry was sometimes resolved by this 'flight' to the unoccupied spaces. This 'flight' should be understood as a search for *another* life whose spatial form is yet to be created. Hence the archetype of a wanderer and wandering; after all, a wanderer is the one who has gained freedom in continuous flight and who refuses the certainty of his final destination; he is a character of pure movement, without stops and shelters, an extratemporal. (See Kirill Chistov, *Russkie narodnye sotsial'no-utopicheskie legendy XVII–XIX* [Russian folk socio-utopian legends of the XVII–XIX centuries], Moscow, 1967, 237–8.)

9 Platonov, *Zapisnye knizhki*, 71.

those who are forever linked to us by bodies, perish. The deserted space is filled up with the invisible. And as long as this space collects the dead and we die without a sense of care for it, the power of the dead over the living will only grow. The invisible must be open to recollection and corporeal transformation. Platonov sensed deeply the artificial split of one life into an invisible one and a visible one. Perhaps, if we look closely, the visible life, by emptying and scattering itself, leaves behind the traces of the invisible, universal forces of life, a life for all. Why do we believe that what died went away irrevocably into the abyss of the invisible? After all, it is sufficient to take a closer look at what is at our feet, as do Platonov's 'most contemplative' heroes, for us to discover the tiniest traces of a once-living experience of life, traces leading to the invisible:

> From around the village he had gathered into it all of the pauper and rejected objects, all the petty oblivion, and all kinds of unconsciousness – for the sake of socialist retribution. This worn down and long-suffering trash had once upon a time touched the flesh and blood of hired landless laborers; in these things the burden of their stooped-over life was imprinted for eternity, life spent without conscious meaning, life which had perished ingloriously and lay somewhere beneath the rye straw of the earth. Voshchev, without completely understanding, had thriftily accumulated in his bag the material remains of lost people, who like him had lived without truth and who had come to their end before the victorious finish. So now he presented these liquidated toilers to the face of the authorities and of the future, in order, by means of organisation of the eternal meaning of people, to obtain retribution – for those who lay quietly in the depths of the earth . . . Instead of people, the activist listed the marks of existence: a bark sandal from the last century, a tin earring from a shepherd's ear, a pantleg of canvas, and various other equipment of the working, yet propertyless, body.[10]

The empty spaces of Platonov's literary works are empty for those who perceive life only in its visible forms and who are indifferent to the fate of the dispersed, tiny particles of that which was once alive. Not whole and visible bodies, but invisible bodies, permeable for myriads of particles of a

---

10   Andrei Platonov, 'The Foundation Pit', trans. Thomas P. Whitney, in *Collected Works*, 131–2.

life that once was. The spaces that the eunuch of the soul observes without trembling are populated with the dead. But, as the dead become invisible, they do not die. The dead are a hallucination from which one has to wake up and which can be overcome. To learn to live outside of one's lonely body that is awaiting death: 'I want to live outside', says Dvanov in one of his dreams, 'I feel cramped in here. . .'[11] This unearthly emptiness of Platonov's landscape frightens the reader; it forms at the limits of the visible and the dead life, unreturned to itself; it leads Sasha Dvanov, the hero of *Chevengur*, to the lake of his childhood, to the old dream, through the mortal split, to the body of the father. By slipping into the dream of death, Dvanov awakens to the invisible life: now neither his body nor his father's body can exist separately, the death is overcome.

> Dvanov urged Proletarian Strength into the water, until it reached the horse's chest. Then, not saying farewell to the horse, continuing his own life, Dvanov got from the saddle into the water himself. He sought that same road along which once his father had passed in his curiosity about death, though Dvanov walked it in a feeling of shame at living in the face of that weak, forgotten body whose remains suffered in the grave because Dvanov remained ever and the same, bearing the same warming traces of his father's existence in a still undestroyed form.[12]

Death is not a limit, it has nothing to delimit, it makes no sense for the invisible, although it remains the highest sign of transition for all visible forms of life. 'To stare death in the face' is not the sort of Stoic valour that we will find among Platonov's heroes. One simply slips into death as into new life. To reach at once the farther horizon where 'man meets man' means to understand death as a path, not as a destination. Moreover, real life is life that transcends death. Life flows out in a multitude of traces, particles and vibrations; it does not attach importance to the death of individual visible bodies, for it is no longer a life that we live as feeling and loving beings who are dying in solitude. The existential status of death is changing. We, the readers of Platonov, cannot always understand this, because we know only one individual death. For only when death is a sign of the special value of life can it be necessarily correlated with the personal structures, with the individual development that

---

11   Platonov, *Chevengur*, 275–6.
12   Ibid., 332.

is determined by our future death. To call myself 'I' means that by this very act of naming I condemn myself to death, and, at the same time, as if forgetting it, continue to see this 'I' as the only force that asserts life and preserves it. By saying 'I', we seek to grasp life in one gesture, believing that 'I' is an existentially evident measure for life. Platonov tries to resist the old opposition *life–death*: death cannot be juxtaposed with life as a rightful part of the oppositional pair. With his death Dvanov crosses over into another life, as if his entire life consisted in a continuation of his dream. It is extremely difficult to understand how one can live a life that forms all unbroken strong connections only at microscopic levels of existence. Because for Platonov's hero to live this life is not to be a human being (to completely lose the image of the body, the measurability, the values and, finally, the History), it means to become new Nature.

In this respect, Platonov's prose has little to do with the traditions of the classic Russian novel, where individual, personal death (Tolstoy's *Death of Ivan Ilyich*) was experienced so intensely. Platonov belonged to another tradition (Gogol, Dostoyevsky, Bely) and did not know how to portray death *from within* – as a final event of life, and as, in principle, understandable to the one who depicted it. Hence the lack of recognition of the existential status of death. The sacred secret of life can be revealed, since the personal principle no longer makes sense in this great struggle against death.[13] And death is no longer death, but a threshold that can be surpassed. Nikolai Fyodorov was the first to make this point: what is dead is what was once alive but is now broken up into the smallest particles and wandering around the earth and cosmos, i.e. a dead being is a potentially living being. What is needed is a rational, targeted effort of gathering the living out of the (allegedly) dead. This is not the place to take a closer look at Fyodorov's entire conception, here we just want to emphasise the

---

13   The famous film director Alexander Sokurov, in a number of early films, attempted to insert this particularly important Platonov requisite – a 'dead body', a non-living body, to put it simply, a march of the corpse – into the centre of the cinematic narrative (in films such as *The Stone, The Second Circle, Mother and Son, Days of Eclipse* and others). I think the director discerned the nature of the heroes of Platonov's novels – they are not just psycho-automatons or marionettes, some sort of mechanical monsters, they are those who have died but who are not dead, who await resurrection. To touch death and to see it entrenched in a non-living body with which kinship ties have not yet been broken is what gives today's living hope that the death will eventually be overcome. All of this is clearly derived from Fyodorov's ideas but without any cosmocratic optimism.

following: if the living shifts to the level of the invisible, then in this shift there is a clear dissatisfaction with the forms of visible life, an artificial life that has lost any connection with the bodies of our fathers. On the other hand, how can it be otherwise when the visible forms are disfigured by the sociality and power that demand that we forget and abandon the legacy of the Fathers? Fyodorov knows the way out: he hopes for another power that can be called *cosmocratic*. But what is preventing this power from *becoming actual*? What does it need to free itself from? From death, of course. But what does that mean? It means to take away death's suffocating oppression over individual bodies, for it not only kills and maims, but also divides, imbues with itself all human relationships with nature as well as a human being's relationship with himself.

But does it also mean freedom from individuation as the process of socialisation and separation from the masses, and the eventual demise of a human being? This figure of the visible life is determined within the limits of death. Life is held in some equilibrium with its environment, but it is held so by the force of death. Here death is correlated with a number of psychical states, and it is experienced not as the death of others, but as death, i.e. it is experienced existentially; my 'I' is just a psycho-reflex of my individual states. The figures of visible human life are eliminated by the 'cosmocratic' myth. The idea of Fyodorov's project of 'The Resurrection of the Dead' was to return to the bodies of the Fathers, to resume a past life, and thus to end a useless waste of life. To create living bodies that no longer require separation from the world, so that one living thing could be another living thing, always without death and therefore without needing to be born. To give life infinite boundaries, another quality; to introduce it into the order of the cosmotelluric science of the future. Now life goes beyond the finite opposition between the living and the dead. 'Death is a property, a state determined by causes, but not a quality without which a person ceases to be what he is and what he should be.'[14] Death is not yet experienced to a point that one might confirm that it is the end of life, and if this is the case, then there is always something that remains beyond the boundary of death *within* which death itself exists. If we assume that a human being retains in himself, in the form of many traces of the past, the biogenetic heritage of his ancestors, then can we not construct a new perfect science on the basis of which the greatest

---

14   Nikolai Fyodorov, *Sobranie sochinenii v chetyryekh tomakh* [Collected works in four volumes], Volume 1, Moscow, 1995, 258.

megamachine of life could be created?[15] On the other hand, technological innovations concern, for example, experiments in managing the high-elevation electrical environment, an invention of the already mentioned cosmotelluric science. This science of life must stand against the blind force of the natural cycle called death. But if death can be eliminated as a phenomenon of life, i.e. extracted from itself due to its organic disintegration into the smallest particles of the myriads of corporeal remains, then we will have a cosmic substance from which we can create anew our own body. In this respect, the longing and the sorrow with which Platonov experiences the insurmountability of death suggests that he does not share Fyodorov's *cosmist* optimism. In sum, the goal is to recreate any sort of body, but also to create for oneself any corporeal appearance; it is clear that we are no longer talking about a personal individual body, its 'mortality' and 'accidentality', but rather about a cosmic *Megamachine*, a collective Body for each and for all (the contradiction between the one and the many, this evil of bourgeois individuation, no longer exists).[16]

Platonov is *ahistorical*, or, to put it slightly differently, he describes a space that no longer needs human time, it increases in emptiness,

---

15   Nikolai Fyodorov, *Sobranie sochinenii v chetyryekh tomakh* [Collected works in four volumes], Volume 2, Moscow, 1995, 271.

16   Here are some of Platonov's 'Fyodorov-like' statements: 'In long solitude Sambikin has stroked the naked body of the dead child – the most sacred property of socialism – and grief had warmed up inside him, a deserted grief that could not be salved by anyone. Toward midnight, with his instruments, he had dug out the heart in the late boy's chest; then he had removed a gland from the area of the throat and begun to investigate these two organs with his devices and preparations, trying to discover where the unspent charge of living energy was being stored. Sambikin was convinced that life is only one of the rare peculiarities of eternally dead matter, and that this peculiarity is concealed where physical substance is more durably structured; this was why the dead needed as little, to return to life, as they had previously needed in order to die. More than that, the vital tension of someone being consumed by death was so great that a sick person is sometimes stronger than a healthy one, while the dead may have more potential for life than the living. Sambikin had decided to use the dead to revive the dead . . .' (Platonov, *Happy Moscow*, 81–2). And in another text: 'He loved machines because he felt them to be alive – they were dead who became living; it was the resurrection of the iron and all that was dead to a life alongside man: an image of the future, fully alive world' (Platonov, *Zapisnye knizhki*, 240). The idea is the same: there is nothing dead anywhere, there is only life, now reduced to a minimum of existence, now deployed in excessive power and might, a supernatural event. Therefore, there is life in the dead itself; it is possible that both in the wood and in the stone, the dead organism remains a part of life. A machine is just that paradoxical case where the dead creates and recreates the living. This is an upside-down mimesis: Nature imitates the Machine (that is new Nature).

awakening in a human being a fatal capacity for the final metabolism, or, more precisely, an *urge to disappear*, a capacity for natural and free transition from the visible world to the invisible world. Such will be the case with renewed nature, nature returned to itself. There are two paths for a human being: first, to again become a natural, non-historical being, simply to be in the world, to be like an animal, a plant, a ray of sunlight; or, second, to become a human-machine, which would naturally bracket out everything that is human (passions, pain, hope, love). Thus, the machine, this new subject of great history, is being given the function of a re-creation of nature on the new foundation. From here, there is continuity in the circulation of transitions from nature (an enemy) to history, and then from history to a new reawakened, 're-created' nature (a friend), but now this nature is 'constructed' and machinic.

The collapse of the *temporal* into the *spatial*, of *History* into *Nature*, is infinite. Some fragments are split up into smaller ones, these, in turn, into more fragments, and these split up again until they become the dust of steppes and deserts. Not ruins but, precisely, the *dust* that marks, for Platonov, the end of History's time. But, in the reverse movement of world-time, it is the ashes, the small, perhaps the smallest and the most invisible, remnants of the substance of life that can form a continuum of the future existence beyond death and time. In Platonov, emptying out is a universal existential, from which we extract all other consequences and skills of existence. To start from a blank page: post-catastrophic time is the time of new people. Just a few figures, almost stationary, with a very limited set of motoric reflexes, and even they are not in space, but are rather fluid configurations, graphic sketches, outlines, shadows on the wall. This is what they look like against the background of stable authorial self-consciousness, the negative tonality that determines everything: the tonality *of emptying out*. A space in which there is less and less human participation can only be emptied out. The world of Platonov's a-topia is deserted, uninhabited; there are no familiar and stable things in it; emptiness and desolation prevail, it is empty of everything and everyone. But why or for what? The answer seems to be along the lines of Fyodorov's ideas: for the sake of *another* world, a world that can be created exclusively by scientific thought, i.e. by the invention of a great Machine of life, which is able to resist Nature that brings death. Platonov did not give anything up, but only thought through to the end that which seemed obvious during the so-called avant-garde period of the development of

Russian literature and art. The revolution is total, therefore those who are coming to succeed current human beings cannot remain the same. Therefore all those who 'made revolution' must now leave the scene of history. Nature returns to itself, bypassing the mediation of humanity, its 'made-up' History. The goal is to reach a limit, but only in order to die. Platonov's experience of the catastrophe is defined by the order of relations existing between the three post-catastrophic *existentials*: *emptying out* (of the world), *exhaustion* (of the body) and *longing/boredom* (of the soul). Properly speaking, this is the summary of Platonov's parable of the time of the Revolution in *Chevengur*.

3

The Inventor of Machines

You know, I accidentally discovered the principle of wireless transmission of energy. But only the principle. Implementation is still far away. If I have time, I will write an article for a scientific journal.[1]

The Parade of Machines

All of these machines that come to us from the pages of Platonov's works (especially during the period of 1920–30s) differ in parameters, place, functions and so on. And yet it seems that they do belong to the same root of imagination, are reflected in one another and create one another. Our notion of Platonov's machines will be arranged by the degree of development in his literary experiments of what can be called *a machinic feeling*. I highlight some of the milestone images of the *machinic mimesis*:

Machinic hymns: this is the poetry of machines; they sing, creak, hit, tear apart; we are excited in the face of this monstrous sacrifice of millions; through pain and torture we acquire a new corporeal form (envy of the machine, terror of the mass castration).

The machinic feeling is *elaborated* in Platonov's fatherly cult of the *steam locomotive*. Here we see the emergence of the phenomenon of machinic

---

1   Andrei Platonov, . . . *Ya prozhil zhizn': Pisma 1920–1950 godov* [I had lived a life: Letters 1920–1950], Moscow, 2016, 240.

totemism (Claude Lévi-Strauss); individual machines are mastered, adapted to human dimensions, and transformed into special technical objects, which can be managed only if one recognises their magical force, a force that one then serves.

Further, machinic feeling subordinates itself to the surge of technical imagination. Platonov, inventor and poet, ameliorator and surveyor, geographer and geologist, engineer and machinist, writes a number of stories and novels in which the first place is occupied by an *ethereal* or a *light* machine (the invention of EMR – *electromagnetic resonator*). It is on this, third, level that we find the greatest machine, whose mission is to free humanity from its eternal struggle for survival. The natural being of humans must be transformed: physically split up and dispersed; here the mimetic, animalistic-totemic feeling of the machine falls into a trap of self-destruction. The machines of this kind reach the deepest layers of matter, they control its birth and energy, while they ruthlessly destroy the Earth and Humankind: the time of global *emptying out* has arrived. . .

This level is opposed by the drive of the proletarian masses toward a 'soft' gradual change of Nature by means of amateur creativity: all kinds of machines-handicrafts are invented, what Deleuze and Guattari called 'machines that don't work'; these are strange embryos of the future amazing technical machines.

The experiment goes further (the fourth level of machinic feeling): Platonov tests the power of another machine on his heroes, a machine that does not need any technical devices or energy. The machinic feeling turns to its own origins: in the human brain, one finds a foundation for the future domination of Nature. Thought itself, by mastering the rhythms of the ethereal (electromagnetic) fields of Cosmos, becomes the greatest of the machines. The time is coming when with even the weakest strains of his mind the human being will be able to stop the movement of planets, change the trajectory of comets, transform the environment, the conditions of labour, and his own nature.

(1) *Dynamo-hymns.* The son of a steam locomotive engineer, Platonov loved machinic devices passionately and was an inventor of various machines. His prose and poetry of the 1920s is imbued with a magical

atmosphere of worship of the machinic civilisation of the future; humans and machines, merging into a single image, become the emblem of the revolutionary era. Let us listen to two such anthems:

> It makes noise, it hums, it is on fire all day long;
> The workshop is full of smoke and dust.
> Servile slaves of machines,
> Their arms and backs bent,
> Work for hours, swallowing dust.
> His head is lowered over his tools,
> Blood flows and forms a trail,
> There stands without memory,
> Looking like a shadow or a dead man,
> A slave with deformed hands.
> Suddenly, he falls. The hand trembles,
> The machine stops whizzing.
> Everyone runs toward him from all sides,
> But he no longer needs help,
> His pain and his life are gone.[2]

> Empty spaces burned away;
> Eternity disappeared in a blink of an eye,
> Immortal wanderers are wandering,
> All mysteries grasped . . .
> Comrade, let us build machines,
> Let us take iron in our iron hands,
> We will explode the worlds in our cylinders,
> We will move the universe from its resting place.
> Light of furnaces is in our eyes,
> Our hearts explode with blood,
> Our souls are red-hot,
> Our song bellows like a factory horn.[3]

---

2   Andrei Platonov, 'Raby mashin' [The slaves of machines], in *Usomnivshyisya Makar. Rasskazy 1920kh godov. Stikhotvoreniya*, 436.

3   Andrei Platonov, 'Sgoreli pustye prostranstva' [Empty spaces burned away], in *Usomnivshyisya Makar. Rasskazy 1920kh godov. Stikhotvoreniya*, 471.

We can see from these poems-hymns that Platonov related to the world of machines with an ambiguous, intensely tragic feeling. On the one hand, machines make us powerless, cripple us and remake our bodies, take away life; they are messengers of the cosmic catastrophe, heroes of apocalyptic narratives. Once he becomes a 'working part', a person is reduced to the position of an automaton that has no choice and no will, he is the 'slave' of the machine. On the other hand, without machines there is no way to create a new society and a new humanity. True, in order to make this possible, a radical rebirth of humanity is required. The poet interprets the machinic nature of the modern world very broadly: the poem itself is a machine that is technically perfect and beautiful.

> Every new machine is a genuine proletarian poem. Every new great labour of changing nature for the sake of humanity is a clear exciting proletarian prose. The greatest danger to our art is the transformation of labour-as-creativity into songs about labour. Electrification – this is the first proletarian novel, our big book in an iron binding. Machines are our poetry and the work of machines is the beginning of the proletarian poetry, which is itself an uprising of humanity against the universe.[4]

The machine as the principle of organisation of the matter of verse, of the entire proletarian poetry. And that means that our soul is a machine, and all that is around us is a hurricane of all-annihilating machinic rhythms. The machine is placed inside the consciousness of the proletariat to serve as an image of the new world.

(2) *Locomotive-(as-a)-totem.* The Proletkult theorists' interest in the machinisation of human existence and everyday life was similar to the renewal of old forms of totemism. Here the totems are technical things of civilisation, different kinds of machines, apparatuses and devices: *dynamo-machines, pumps, automobiles, motorcycles, steam locomotives,*

---

4   Platonov, 'Proletarskaya poeziia' [Proletarian poetry], 167. See also the following: 'And I propose that we organise an evening dedicated to a yet unborn poet of the future who is already weaving the iron crowns of his songs. His name is the Machine. The machine chews the world and creates a joyful song from sadness like the Russian people on the Volga. But the sounds of its song are not quivering words, but transformed worlds, a dancing cosmos. I suggest we have an evening dedicated to the poet-machine, a comrade to all of us. I am volunteering to be a presenter' (ibid., 178–9).

electromagnetic resonators, '*ethereal tunnels*' and so on. The totem (machine) is *a thing* that is endowed with supernatural power, the nature of which cannot be known to those who entrust it with their destiny. The totemic or magical practice of Platonov's characters-workers is fully consistent with the idea of labour economy of life, or, at least, it does not limit it in any way. The first scene of the contact between humans and machines: in the magical spiritualisation of the machine, the body, becoming the body of the machine, ceases to be human; it is already a machine-beast, a natural element of machinism, and, as a consequence, the reincarnation of the human corporeality. There are many characters that sense 'machinic mechanisms as accurately as their own flesh': 'Frosya's husband had the ability to respond to the tension of the electric current as a personal passion. Touched by his hands or his thoughts, things came to life, and he, therefore, acquired a genuine understanding of the flow of force in any mechanical device and was directly affected by the resistance patiently endured by the metal body of the machine.'[5] Or in another passage: 'He loved machines because he felt that they were alive – dead things that came to life; it was the resurrection of metal and of all that was dead for a human life: an image of the future, a fully living world.'[6] Or this: 'Zh(ovov) treated iron like his own flesh, better than his own body.'[7] Or, finally, this:

> During lunch breaks Zakhar Pavlovich would not take his eyes from the engine, silently suffering within himself his love for it. He carried back to his quarters bolts, old valves, faucets, and other mechanical items. He arranged them in a row on the table and surrendered himself to staring at them, never growing dull from solitude. In fact Zakhar Pavlovich was not solitary – machines were his people, constantly arousing within him feelings, thoughts, and desires. The forward slope of the engine, which they called the spool, forced Zakhar Pavlovich to worry about the infinity of space.[8]

We could provide many more examples. In this scene of the first magical contact with the machine we see the merger of the human body

---

5 Andrei Platonov, 'Fro', trans. Alexey A. Kiselev, in *Collected Works*, 375.
6 Platonov, *Zapisnye knizhki*, 240.
7 Ibid., 106.
8 Platonov, *Chevengur*, 27.

with the body of the machine. This is not a substitution, but rather *an incarnation* of the human in the machinic form: the machine is domesticated, becomes equal to and yet above human being; the machine is the true human being of the future. 'Revolution is like a locomotive. And revolutionaries must be machinists.'[9] Is that not who the machinist Mal'tsev is – the man-locomotive from the novella *In a Beautiful and Violent World*? And what about the master Pukhov from *The Innermost Man*? This way the machine-locomotive becomes a 'warm-blooded beast'. 'The locomotive stood magnanimous, enormous, and warm in the harmonious swales of its high majestic body. The foreman concentrated, sensing the ringing involuntary awe within him.'[10] Because of the introduction of the machine, all problems of human existence are solved at once: the machine becomes the new Nature. The machine-beast, the beast-machine. In other words, by transforming its machinic sense into a mimesis of the beastly (the animal-natural), the human being domesticates the machine. He does not become a machine, but rather turns the machine into one of the natural phenomena.

In one case, the human is part of the *machine-as-a-whole*; the desire is not even to become the machine – that is an unattainable and impossible happiness – but to belong, at least partly, to its power and beauty, as one can belong to the Supreme Being; a living organic 'part' is eager to become a mechanical whole. In Platonov's *atopia* machines do not take the place of human beings, but the place of Nature; the machine-locomotive is a special kind of bio-hybridisation of a technical device and human flesh. Therefore, there is nothing mysterious about a bear from *The Foundation Pit* who is a blacksmith's striker and is also actively involved in collectivisation.[11] That is how the animal-plant order of machinic metaphors is formed, and this is what constitutes domestication – 'the taming of the Machine'. The reason for the literary machinisation of the world is the desire to become the Other: to achieve a certain affective state which is projected onto the world by means of various technical objects, forms and constructions; they are individualised, taken out of the range of accepted norms of technological progress (i.e. pulled out of their social context), to become fantastic machines in which the reality of the future is folded

---

9   Andrei Platonov, *Povesti i rasskazy* [Novels and short stories], Moscow, 1988, 105.

10   Platonov, *Chevengur*, 28.

11   Platonov, 'The Foundation Pit', 119.

up. Although Platonov's machines belong to different classes and types of the avant-garde machinism, they are all affective (mimetic) devices.

(3) *Ethereal, electromagnetic or light machine.* Platonov's favourite machine is a machine of light, an electric machine that captures the low-cost invisible ethereal energy. This machine was invented by Dvanov (in *Chevengur*), Vogulov (in *The Satan of Thought*), the worker in *Markun*, the main hero of *The Impossible*, Kreitskopf (in *The Lunar Bomb*), Popov and Kirpitchnikov (in *Ethereal Tract*), Vermo (in *The Juvenile Sea*), Ivan Koptchikov (in *The Story about Many Interesting Things*), the character from *The Descendants of the Sun*, and Elpidifor Baklazhanov from *The Adventures of Baklazhanov*. And how could one not love this machine, if, according to its creators' intention, it had to become a real embodiment of the amazing possibilities of human reason? The machine's amazing power would come from using the most powerful forces of the Cosmos, forces capable of giving life and everything that exists a new dimension – *electromagnetic forces* – the 'living' energy of the dead substance of nature. All of these machines which captured Platonov's imagination were indisputably related to the scientific discoveries and inventions of his time, especially in the field of electrical engineering. And here we see the figure of the brilliant scientist Nikola Tesla, whose works, it seems safe to assume, Platonov knew. Virtually all the ideas expressed by Platonov's heroes resemble artistically reworked ideas of Tesla. The magical philosophy of technology, characteristic of Tesla, coincides with the details of Platonov's thoughts and projects (various types of electric machines, devices and instruments).

The great goal is to acquire the energy of 'dead' nature, the cheapest and the most inexhaustible energy. The greatest and most powerful energy lies at the heart of matter; its discovery and proper use would make it possible to eliminate the boundaries between the isolated times of the global substance, between heaven and earth, woman and man, living and dead, father and son. The rejection of the 'curse' of labour as a useless expenditure of human abilities, as a form of mutual exploitation of workers. This is a machine of height/depth; it goes all the way up into Cosmos; it penetrates the depths of the Earth. This depth is not emptiness, but a path to cheap ethereal energy. This machine of life works vertically: it is an elevator tunnel, with the help of which the products of the activity of pure forces of matter are extracted to the surface of the Earth. Platonov, in describing his strange and amazing machines, often uses biological metaphors that seem to encourage us to see in these machines not rigid mechanisms with limited scope of action, but rather orgasmic pulsations. This is a type of machine-phantasm: dreamlike machines, super-productive machines that 'do not know death'. However, in its reverse projection, the ethereal machine as the machine of life coincides in its functions with the machines of death. Transferred onto a horizontal plane, for example, the ethereal machine is no different from the machines of terrorism, violence and impoverishment. One object of the application of power is replaced by another, the human body by the body of the Earth. The basic principle of action remains unchanged: to extract energy from the passive natural body and to consume it in increasing quantities, without worrying about the cosmic unity of human beings and Earth.

(4) *Cerebral machine.* Platonov's anti-utopian novels view technology (the entire fleet of machines and automatons) as the necessary condition of the revolutionary changes that capture Nature and continue on to radically change humanity. In terms of the new cosmic ontology, as a renewed theory of *macro-and-microcosmos*, a human being is just a machine – reasonable and conscious, but still a machine. The great inventor wrote: 'I am an automaton endowed with power of movement, which merely responds to external stimuli beating upon my sense organs and thinks and acts and moves accordingly.'[12] The hypothesis of a 'living universe' that finds itself in a continuous, oscillating wave environment (an electromagnetic environment) implies the presence of a single universal consciousness that cannot be individualised, i.e. appropriated. A human being is a psycho-automaton whose relationship with the world is built thanks to his *reactivity*, i.e. his ability to successfully respond to external stimuli. More than that, a human being is just a brain, but this brain is a thought, and the thought, if it is correct, resonates with the infinite world of other resonations; thus, the thought is the rhythm of the universe. For example:

Sartorius had spent all his youth in the study of physics and mechanics; he has labored over the computation of infinity as a body, trying to find

12   Nikola Tesla, 'The Problem of Increasing Human Energy', *The Century Illustrated Monthly Magazine* (June 1900), 188 [175–211].

an economical principle of its actions. He has wanted to discover, in the very flow of human consciousness, a thought that worked in resonance with nature and so – even if only by chance, by virtue of living chance – reflected the whole of nature's truth; and he had hoped to secure this thought forever through some calculable formula.[13]

And elsewhere: 'Matissen's brain was a mysterious machine, which gave new montage to the depths of space, and the apparatus on the table moved this brain to action. Ordinary human thoughts, normal movements of the brain, are powerless to influence the world, which requires vortexes of brain particles – only then will the world's material be shaken by a storm.'[14] Platonov does not 'make things up', but merely tries to match in his machinic fantasies the revolutionary acceleration of technological progress. And he was not alone.

Malevich left a curious theory of machinism, which renewed the avant-garde's perception of the world. It placed the human brain at the very tip of machinic progress: 'am I not the new terrestrial skull in whose brain the new flowering takes place, is not my brain the foundry from which the new transfigured world of iron flows, and from which lives, which we call inventions, take wing, as if from the hive of universality?'[15] The brain, if presented from a different terminological perspective, is intuition. Malevich defines it in the following way: 'Intuition is the kernel of infinity. Everything that is visible on our globe disperses in it. Forms originated from the intuitive energy which conquers the infinite. Hence arise variants of form as tools of movement.'[16] Intuition is the radical renewal of the world in action, it is thought itself, and, in the face of this thought, the world is nameless and subordinated only to the speed of the tools of overcoming. And here, like in Platonov, the machinic activity comes down to the *dispersion* of matter. The great avant-garde impulse is to increase the might of the tools for overcoming Nature (for splitting it into particles, into 'grains of infinite thought'). Only thought is proportional to the infinity of the task; the ever-renewing technical world is only a collection of tools for overcoming, each one revealing the dynamic might of human reason in the cosmic infinity of new worlds. Machines

---

13   Platonov, *Happy Moscow*, 49.
14   Platonov, *Efirnyi trakt*, 64.
15   Malevich, 'On New Systems in Art', in *Essays on Art, Volume 1*, 86–8 [83–117].
16   Ibid., 104.

approach the 'end of time'; these are catastrophic machines, 'machines of death', despotically extracting energy from everything (including human bodies) and dispersing it again.

(5) *Machines-handicrafts*. Many of Platonov's works are experimental testing grounds for the idea of immortality, from 'perpetuum mobile' devices to various instruments and contraptions without discernible practical uses. Thus, there are many of the most unusual machinic devices, which can be called *machines-handicrafts*.

> He was not unduly interested in anything, not in people or nature, except for mechanical things of all sorts. Because of this he regarded people and fields with indifferent tenderness, not infringing upon the interests of either. On winter evenings he occasionally made unnecessary things such as towers of wire, ships cut from pieces of roofing tin, paper dirigibles, and so on, exclusively for his own pleasure. It often happened that he even delayed filling someone's chance commission, so that, for example, when he was given a vat to fix with new handles, he spent the time instead building a wooden clock which he intended to run without works, powered just by the rotation of the earth.[17]

> Now Yepishka invented light. He created such magnets where daylight disturbed the magnetic field and produced electric current. With this current, Yepishka powered a *homemade ship* along his native river. For the first time ever, sunlight and lunar light were moving an eccentric man along the river. Since then, no one needed anyone else: Yepishka showed everyone how to make such machines, and everyone became rich . . . One resident of Ararat created an *underground boat*, and the power of Yepishka's machine drove the boat into the ground, and the resident of Ararat disappeared in the ground, and decided to live down there.[18]

> Dvanov had thought up an invention which would turn sunlight into electricity. To help Gopner took all the mirrors in Chevengur out of their frames and also collected all the glass that had the least bit

---

17   Platonov, *Chevengur*, 3.

18   Andrei Platonov, 'Izobretatel' sveta' [The inventor of light], in *Usomnivshyisya Makar. Rasskazy 1920kh godov. Stikhotvoreniya*, 313–14.

of thickness to it. With these materials Dvanov and Gopner made complex prisms and reflectors which would transform the sunlight as it passed through them, at the rear of the device yielding an electric current. The device had been ready two days before, but it had not produced electricity. The miscellaneous came by to look over Dvanov's light machine and even though it did not work they decided as they saw necessary, considering the machine correct and vital, for it had been invented and made by the corporeal labor of two comrades.[19]

When Baudrillard called these strange objects *gizmos* [*le machin*], he pointed to the opposition *machine/gizmo*:[20]

The machine [*la machine*] and the gizmo [*le machin*] are mutually exclusive. And it is not that the machine is a perfected form, not that the gizmo is a degraded one: rather, the two are different in kind, the first operating in the real, the second in the imaginary realm. 'Machine' signifies, and in so doing structures, a particular real practical whole; 'gizmo' signifies nothing more than a formal operation – though that operation is the *total* operation of the world. The virtue of a gizmo may be ridiculous in reality, but in the imagination it is universal.[21]

Anything that does not have a name can be called a 'gizmo'. In other words, a thing whose purpose I do not know (but believe it has some use) is a gizmo. Therefore, if I had suddenly remembered the gizmo's *name*, expressions and a dictionary of terms connected with this thing, it would cease being a gizmo and would become a work of art or a technical device.

---

19   Platonov, *Chevengur*, 309.

20   See the following comment by Lévi-Strauss: 'These assimilations are not so extraordinary; we do the same types of assimilating, doubtless more guardedly, when we qualify an unknown object, or one whose function is unclear, or whose effectiveness amazes us, by the French terms *truc* or *machin*. Behind *machin* is machine, and, further back, the idea of force or power. As for *truc*, the etymologists derive it from a medieval term which signifies the lucky move in games of skill or games of chance. . .' (Claude Lévi-Strauss, *Introduction to the Work of Marcel Mauss*, trans. Felicity Baker, London: Routledge & Kegan Paul, 1950, 55).

21   Jean Baudrillard, *The System of Objects*, trans. James Benedict, London: Verso, 2005, 125. We can go further. For it is clear that all the machines that 'do not work', invented mostly by the surrealists, were precisely such 'gizmos'. These were the machines of Léger, Duchamp, Kafka, Burroughs or Warhol, but also all the fantastic machines of the Russian avant-garde.

A gizmo then is a breakdown of memory or of speech. This is the first step, and then there is the second step: a gizmo is also a game of technical fantasy; it is not this gizmo that 'doesn't work' but another gizmo that is the highest form of future technical perfection (for example, an unidentified flying object). Such gizmos are special technical constructions of the future, whose purpose we cannot explain. In that case, the gizmo negates the principle of reality, surpasses it. There is also something that can be called libidinous excess in the explanation of the phenomenon of a gizmo when it suddenly becomes a part of the phallic dimension of the world of objects. Paradoxically, all these primitive contraptions, these machines of Chevengur, having turned into things, become gizmos whose purpose conflicts with their technical uselessness ('they don't work'). In the Russian avant-garde there are no 'gizmos', everything is transparent there: the thing is reduced to an ideal cause, to a particular model (exemplar, mould): *modulor* (Le Corbusier), *architekton* (Malevich). The Russian avant-garde really does strive to create a world-machine, and with its help to rebuild not only human society, but the Cosmos itself.

From the series of engravings by Paul Gustave Doré (1832–83) for Charles Perrault's 'Sleeping Beauty'

From the series of engravings by Paul Gustave Doré (1832–83) for Charles Perrault's 'Sleeping Beauty'

PART II

The Fainting of the World

Poetics of Chance in the
Literature of Oberiu

Introduction

Fear of High Noon

To interrupt the course of the world – that was Baudelaire's deepest intention. The intention of Joshua. Not so much the prophetic one, for he gave no thought to any sort of reform. From this intention sprang his violence, his impatience, and his anger; from it, too, sprang the ever-renewed attempts to stab the world in the heart or sing it to sleep. In this intention he provides death with an accompaniment: his encouragement of its work.[1]

When the time stops, I will stop as well. But if the time does not stop, then my flow will continue uninterrupted.[2]

Scene 1: Catalepsy

There is a particular fear of high noon, when brightness, silence and heat are approaching the limit, when Pan plays his flute, when the

---

1   Walter Benjamin, *The Writer of Modern Life: Essays on Charles Baudelaire*, trans. Howard Eiland, Edmund Jephcott, Rodney Livingston and Harry Zohn, Cambridge, MA: The Belknap Press of Harvard University Press, 2006, 145.

2   Daniil Kharms, 'Piat' neokonchennykh povestvovanii' [Five unfinished narratives], in *Polnoe sobranie sochinenii* [Complete collected works], Volume 4, St Petersburg, 2001, 27.

day reaches its full incandescence. On such a day, you walk through a meadow or through a small forest without thinking of anything. Butterflies fly carelessly about you, ants cross your path, and grasshoppers jump sideways from underneath your feet. Flowers amaze you with their smell: how beautiful, intense and free their life is! It is as if they are retreating before everything, giving way out of politeness, and then leaning back into their place. No one is around, and the only sound that accompanies you is the sound of your own beating heart. Warmth and bliss, as in a bathtub. The day stands at its highest, happiest point . . .

Suddenly, an anticipation of irreparable misfortune grips you: time is getting ready to stop. The day is growing heavy with lead. The catalepsy of time! The world stands before you as a muscle compressed with convulsion, like a pupil of an eye frozen from pressure. My God, what hollow motionlessness, what deadly blossoming all around! The bird flies in the sky and you notice with horror: its flight is motionless. A dragonfly caught a gnat and is chewing on its head; and both of them, the dragonfly and the gnat, are completely motionless. *How have I not noticed until now, that nothing is happening in the world, and that nothing can happen, it has been like this and will be like this for ever and ever.* And there is neither now, nor before, nor for ever and ever. Now if only I can avoid realising that I am also fossilised, because then it's all over, there's no going back. *Is there no salvation from the enchanted world? Will the frozen pupil swallow me as well? Horrified and disquieted you wait for the liberating explosion. And the explosion bursts out.*

– *The explosion bursts out?*

– *Yes, someone's calling you by name.*

Gogol wrote something about this. The ancient Greeks knew that feeling, too. They called it a meeting with Pan, a panic horror. It is a fear of high noon.[3]

Yes, you are in standing water. A solid cover of water that closes over your head like a stone. It happens where there is no distinction, no change, no sequence. For example, a busy day, where light, smell and extreme heat stand like thick rays, like horns. A solid world without gaps, without time, without pores, and there is no diversity in it, and

---

3   Leonid Lipavsky, *Issledovanie uzhasa* [The study of horror], Moscow, 2005, 21.

therefore there is no time; individuality cannot exist in it. Because if everything is the same, everything is immeasurable. There are no differences, nothing exists.

But then who was it that at the last moment called you by your name? It was you yourself, of course. In mortal fear, you remembered the last denominator, you remembered about yourself, and you grabbed your soul with both hands.[4]

Scene 2: A Plant

I want to know who came up with a fairy tale about a sleeping kingdom. I mean, there must have been someone who invented it, who first came up with this strange thought. And obviously, he touched a nerve since this fairy tale made an impression on everyone, it spread all over the world.

Remember, in this fairy tale even the clock stops, a servant freezes in his course, still putting his foot forward and holding a plate in one hand. And at once, trees rise from the ground, grasses grow long like hair, and everything around is covered with something like green spiderweb or green yarn. Yes, there's also an attic with a hearing window, an angry old woman who is weaving, and a sleeping beauty: she fell asleep because she pricked her finger, and a little blood came out.[5]

What is the role of the finger prick? What is its connection with the cessation of time, with sleep?

But, first, let us ask about the yarn. It is said that yarn is reminiscent of fate; but it is even more reminiscent of a plant. Like a plant, it has no centre and is infinite, unlimited in its course. There is boredom in it; there is time, not filled with anything; there is common, ancestral life that branches out again and again for no apparent reason; when you are trying to remember it, you do not know whether it existed or not, it

---

4   Ibid., 22.

5   Cf. Charles Perrault, *The Complete Fairy Tales*, trans. Christopher Betts, Oxford: Oxford University Press, 2009, 86–7. We should mention other fairy tales, for example, the retelling of Perrault's fairy tale by Pushkin in his *The Tale of the Dead Princess and Seven Knights*, as well as *Snow White and the Seven Dwarves* by the Grimm brothers. In these versions the same plot line remains: an apple, an act of poisoning, a drop of blood, lethargic sleep, and a number of other supplementary elements.

slipped through your fingers, passed by like an infinite blink of an eye, like a dream, leaving nothing to remember.

It is curious that until today many people are afraid of the sight of blood, and they feel sick when they see it. And what, one might ask, is so frightening about it? Here it comes through a cut, a bit of red moisture that contains life, it flows freely and slowly, it spreads into an undefined, ever-expanding stain. Although, perhaps, there is something unpleasant about that. The blood leaves its home too simply and easily and becomes a separate warm puddle, it is impossible to tell whether it is alive or dead. Whoever watches it, thinks it is so unnatural that he grows weak, the world in his eyes turns into a grey feculence, a dizzying longing. In fact, something unnatural and abhorrent is taking place here, like a tickle coming not from the outside, but taking place in the depths of the body, in its innards. Slowly leaving captivity, blood begins its impersonal life that is truly alien to us; it lives like trees or grass – a red plant among green plants.

Thus, we see that our body is a half-plant: all of its innards are plants.

But impersonal life does not have time; in it, there are no coincidences and impulses. And the plants are different from the animals in this lack of time: everything for them flows into a single infinite blink of an eye, like a sip, like the sound of a pitchfork.

This is the source of the fear of blood, of the disgust that many people feel about it: the fear of unconcentrated life.

A prick of a needle and the intimate link between the elements and the private life is broken; blood streams into an opening; it begins to bloom strangely; the world faints and falls into timeless sleep. And now everything is already covered over, as if with a yarn or a spider-web, by an alien silent green life. The world is once again turning into what it is, into a plant. It grows wildly and motionlessly! It was like this and will always be like this, for ever and ever, until suddenly a creator of a new non-uniformity comes and brings his kiss, then the illusion of something happening will return.[6]

---

6   Lipavsky, *Issledovanie uzhasa*, 23–5.

Scene 3: Time

Let us begin with a famous thought experiment: the whole world and everything in it suddenly stopped, everything froze like in a fairy tale about the sleeping beauty. Here is the question: does this stagnant, enduring world have time or is it timeless?

It is possible that some might think that even in this situation time is preserved. But they make this mistake because when they imagine this situation, they forget to turn off their own individuality, its changeability. And then we see the same thing that happens when one is bored, the discrepancy between the external situation and the course of the individual's acute sense of time creates a sense of longing the same way as when one feels the air more sharply when one is lacking it, when one is suffocating.

But in this experiment, of course, we must turn off or stop all mechanisms, even the mechanisms of our own souls.

And then, if this unfamiliar effort of imagination is made, it will become clear: the enduring world is timeless.

This means that time, like some alien force, like a river that carries the world, is only an emblem. In reality, time is a certain relationship within the world.[7]

Let us imagine that everything in the world, without exception, stopped, froze, came to a halt, like in a fairy tale about the sleeping beauty, when she pricked her finger with a needle. In order that we do not inconspicuously introduce internal changes, let us imagine that we ourselves fell asleep with all other beings and objects, or, at the very least, we fell into a state of being absent, a state in which a person stares at something and loses a sense of himself. We ask the following question: will time flow in this lethargic world?

In order to find the answer, let us imagine that the world woke up and is moving again. If the interruption can be noticed by any, if only indirect, signs, then the time did not stop flowing inside the pause and it was empty time. If, however, there are no and there cannot be any such signs, then the very notion of an enduring interruption of events is a fictitious notion, and the notion of empty time is nonsensical.

---

7 Ibid., 44.

So, someone comes to, wakes up at the same time as the world. If it were a normal dream, one could detect that and discern the duration of the dream by the movement of shadows, the change of light, the disappearance of the feeling of fatigue, the special sensation one has after waking up from a dream – in short, by external or internal transformations. But in our case, nothing like this takes place or can take place. The person in question could not notice a pause, not because he does not have correct means of doing so, but because it is fundamentally impossible. No creature in the world could have noticed the pause, and no object would possess any sign to indicate that the time did flow during the pause.

In short, if anyone would still insist that time existed during this pause, then the answer should be the following: it existed exactly as if it did not exist; there were no signs of its existence. But then time becomes a word without content, a fictitious notion.

That is how one solves the problem of the possibility of an empty time that exists in and of itself.[8]

Scene 4: The World's Cadaver

> The dining table lets survey
> the world cadaver's crème brûlée.
> It stinks of rot around.
> Some dummies practice
> multiplication,
> others drink poison.
> The dry sun, light, and comets
> silently sat down on objects.
> Oaks lowered their crowns.
> The air smelled abject.
> Motion, heat, and density
> have lost their intensity.
> Hope flaps its shivering wing
> alone above the human world.
> A sparrow by a pistol hurled
> barely holds the tips of ideas in its beak.
> Everybody's gone insane.

---

8   Ibid., 68–9.

The world went out like a candle,
the world went out like a rooster.
However, much benefit ensued.
Of course the world still hasn't come to an end,
its crown not bare yet,
but it really has lost a lot of its lustre.
Fomine lay prone and turning blue.
He raised his double-windowed arm
and started praying. Only God may be.
Space lay down far away.
The flight of an eagle flowed above a river.
The eagle held an icon in its fist,
there was God on it.
It may be that sleep made earth
deserted, poor, thin.
It may be we're culprits. We are afraid.
And you airplane eagle may
flash like an arrow into the ocean
or like a sooty candle
collapse into the river.
The star of meaninglessness shines,
it alone is fathomless.
A dead gentleman runs in
and silently removes time.[9]

These fragments are only a small part of the Oberiu archive,[10] where we find an image of the stopped 'world-time'; we can easily assemble these fragments into 'scenes'; there are four of them. The *first* scene captures the fear of high noon, the fear of the instantaneous, the stunning, the frightening – no one has enough time to become brave; 'time is preparing to stop' – the fear grows, the time of high noon is approaching. Here is what else one needs to know about the panic and the panic fear:

---

9   Alexander Vvedensky, *An Invitation for Me to Think*, trans. Eugene Ostashevsky, New York: New York Review of Books, 2013, 65.

10   OBERIU, or OBeRIu, stands for 'Ob'edinenie real'nogo iskusstva' [The union of real art]. In English-language literature it is rendered both in all caps as 'OBERIU' and as 'Oberiu'. We have selected the latter version here. – *Trans.*

He is a guest from Arcadia, of comparatively recent adoption into the assembly of the gods of Greece as a whole, the fantastic guardian spirit of goats, Pan the goat-legged. If we call him a 'god', it is simply because we designate by that name any powerful, immortal being of whatever sort; in reality we understand perfectly the difference between him and the great gods of Olympus. Later the evil conscience of a religion which has cut loose from nature and Mother Earth will change him into the devil; but we love him and respect him as the kindly god of the mountains with the melodious pipes. To be sure, we know of many of his strange pranks, not to speak of those of which his neighbours the oreads might tell us. At noonday he takes a nap (that is 'the hour of Pan'), and woe to the incautious shepherd who ventures at that time to amuse himself by playing his pipes! When the awakened Pan thrusts forth his shaggy brow from behind a crag, when he shouts over all the countryside, then the frightened goats will rush downward over the stones, overturning in their path both one another and the error-stricken shepherd. Never will he forget Pan and his 'panic' fear![11]

Pan's scream awakens to life; it gives a name; it is capable of bringing us back from the deepest dream, the dream where we become dead.

The *second* scene refers to the image of time in Perrault's *Sleeping Beauty*. Time is 'frozen', there are no longer those who perceive it, there is no longer anyone who lives in it. The sign of time's cessation is the growth of plants. Everything grows over with odd flowers and grasses; the princess's scarlet blood flows from a small cut on her finger (an evil witch's doing) and nourishes plants with its power. Everything submerges into a natural unity, into a strange dream; everything becomes one Plant; no one knows how long one will have to wait until the living breath touches the sleeping beauty, until the sleeping world again fills up with the time of life.

When the princess was in trouble, the good enchantress who saved her life by letting her fall asleep for a hundred years was in the kingdom of Mataquin, twelve thousand miles away, but she was instantly informed by a dwarf wearing seven-mile boots (the boots in which seven miles could be covered in one step). The enchantress immediately set off

---

11 Thaddeus Zielinski, *The Religion of Ancient Greece: An Outline*, trans. George Rapall Noyes, Oxford: Oxford University Press, 1926, 23.

on her journey. And an hour later, she was already approaching the castle in a fire chariot, driven by dragons. The king came out to greet her and helped her off the chariot. She approved of everything he had done so far, but, being particularly cautious, thought that the princess, when the time came for her to wake up, would find it difficult to be alone in the old castle. And here is what she did. With her wand, she touched everything in the castle (except the king and the queen): servants, ladies in waiting, chambermaids, cavaliers, butlers, cooks, kitchen boys, errand boys, guards, gatekeepers, pages and lackeys; she also touched all the horses that were standing in the stables, and all the stable attendants, all the large guard dogs, and the little Puff, the princess's dog who was lying with her in bed. As soon as she touched them all, they fell asleep so that they could all wake up with their lady, ready to serve her when needed. The skewer in the fireplace, still full of chickens and pheasants, dozed off as well, and the fire too. All this happened in a blink of an eye: the enchantress worked fast.[12]

The magic wand is the living time that animates the human that was previously frozen in nature. The movement and growth of plants do not show any evidence of time, plants exist outside of time.

The *third* scene is about the representation of time that has suddenly lost its subject. If there is no perception of time (i.e. there is no subject that perceives it), then time itself does not exist. Let us assume that two teams play a game within a strictly measured time frame. Now a coach of one of them takes a time-out, a short break to analyse the current game situation. The game time is suspended, but not stopped completely. The pause in one time allows one to transfer into another time that also has its own limits and also happens within the rules of the game (for example, the rules regarding the length of game interruptions). It is an interesting moment, in some ways similar to the linguistic effect of presupposition. Vis-à-vis the main time of the game, a time-out is a pause (a reprieve, a minute of rest). The game is stopped, and nothing else takes place. But since a time-out, a break, is linked to the general rules of the game, it also acquires a certain meaning within the context of the game. Human time is introduced into the world by an interruption. Is it the case that when a game is stopped, the function of time is passed on to the break that is

---

12   Lipavsky, *Issledovanie uzhasa*, 20–1.

filled up with its own time that is not the *actual* time of the game? In the
course of the game, out of tactical considerations, time-outs, pauses, necessary stops are used in order to reduce the negative impact of the game
on us. In sum, a pause is a time without time; 'let us assume', Lipavsky
notes, 'that the pause has occurred, but that it is inside the world, and
cannot be characterised by time'.[13] At the same time the game itself is a
time-out from the world of everyday life, from the being of everything
existent, as Heidegger would say. A time-out as a 'reprieve', as a return to
regular time, a time of boredom, of being bored, of doing-nothing. Any
limited temporality appears as a time-out from another (conditionally)
unlimited temporality. In the game, humanity imitates Nature (Cosmos),
in a pause and an interruption – only itself. Human time is a downward
cascade of pauses and interruptions.

Finally, in the *fourth* scene, the poet attempts to 'capture' the cessation
of time in the fabric of the verse itself, sensing it with his own skin; he
needs precisely such metaphors in order to stop time, to slow it down, to
force it to disintegrate, to blind us with flashes of nonsense. Is this not an
attempt to translate an internal state of catalepsy into a verse form (into
a refined selection of metaphors, which hang all around the poet like
garlands and do not let him breath)? 'The dining table lets survey / the
world cadaver's crème brûlée'. 'A dead gentleman runs in / and silently
removes time'. 'The world went out like a candle, / the world went out
like a rooster'.[14] The selected fragment describes one state of the world –
its cessation. Something stopped, something else is coming to a stop,
and the next thing is getting ready to begin stopping. The cessation of
the world/time forms what I call a *mimetic axis* of the poetic substance,
its oscillating nerve; this is the way the sorcerous yarn of the fairy tale
grows, thread by thread. The reality of time is perceived by the members
of Oberiu in terms of these slowdowns, folds, moments of cooling off,
falls of images and situations of life. Time flows into the sand, flows out
of things and events, out of familiar gestures and movements – out of
everything, like blood or water. All things come to a stop, some earlier,
some later. The poet is the first witness of the beginning of the cessation
of the world-time.

It is obvious that the real reconstruction of this theme would hardly
be possible without reference to the main works of Yakov Druskin. In my

---

13   Ibid., 71.
14   Vvedensky, *An Invitation for Me to Think*, 65.

opinion, he had every right to the posthumous consolidation of the group into one 'authorial' organism. There were good reasons for that. Above all, the philosophically orientated positions of the members of Oberiu themselves, as formulated by Lipavsky, Kharms and Vvedensky, and later, in a more detailed and systematic form, elaborated by Druskin. The behaviour of the poetic system during its development is unpredictable for an observer. Only *post festum*, when this development is interrupted (no matter how, naturally or tragically), can one raise the question of the virtual form of the (literary) Work. A traditional philosopher always stands face to face with what he calls the Unfathomable, the Primal or the Absolute – it has many names; he is always face to face with an event that generates the initial movement of thought. That is why there is so much that is meaningless and absurd, paradoxical and random, in philosophy – all that has remained unexplained in one system of ideas. And many new explanations are needed in order to deal with the event of thought that took place a long time ago. Other philosophies are needed. Each philosophy tries to provide a logical explanation for what it already understands. In philosophy, understanding precedes explanation: we understand first and explain to ourselves what we understand later. When a philosopher is first exposed to the poetic experience, he again begins with the understanding. We notice, however, that as we begin to explain, our understanding often begins to elude us. And this means that by studying the texts of this or that poetic tradition (repetitions, contrasts and other figures of speech), the philosopher begins to assume the existence of a very valuable idea that must lie at the foundation of poetic ontology. Otherwise, how would poetry be possible?

For the members of Oberiu, such a valuable poetic idea was the theme of the cessation of world-time. Only if we understand this theme can we explain the structure of Oberiu's poetic work. Druskin's extensive commentaries on the works of Vvedensky and Kharms, and his own systematic philosophy, give us a model of this understanding: 'I sense Vvedensky's world quite existentially, that is, I feel it. He is close to me, but still he is a hieroglyph of his poem's last line – 'A man on the wallpaper / but a Thursday on a plate' – I cannot define it and cannot tell you anything about it. Maybe there is no need to say anything here, it is the last limit of thought; and I feel it.'[15] On the one hand, Druskin claims the right to

---

15   Yakov Druskin, *Dnevniki, 1963–1979* [Diaries, 1963–1979], St Petersburg, 2001, 455.

continue the work of Oberiu, and looks at his own way of thinking exclusively from the point of view of the 'Chinar' language:

> Chinar language is atonality, that is, fixation of ontological meaninglessness: linguistic, logical and situational. This fixation of meaninglessness enters my philosophy and theology as the establishment of a real ontological and epistemological antinomy – an identity of aporia or a synthetically one-sided identity, then as antinomy of an act and a state, a what and a how, a having and an assimilation, a contemplation and a participation and so on. In this sense, at least to some extent, my philosophy is written in chinar language.[16]

On the other hand, Druskin considers himself the 'last member of Oberiu' who recognises the influence of friends who were gone before their time, though he does not tire of stressing the self-sufficiency of his own philosophical position, defending his ideas in an indirect dispute with thinkers like Wittgenstein, Heidegger, Husserl and others.

---

16   Ibid., 320–1. ('Chinari' was an informal literary group that included Druskin, Kharms, Vvedensky and Lipavsky. – *Trans.*)

4

Alea

A General Theory of Chance

Chance, or randomness, is an unaccountable and causeless principle for those who do not believe in providence.[1]

The Choice of Strategies

Among the themes of poetic ontology that inspired Oberiu there is one that determines everything – the theme of *chance*.[2] What is its nature, function and place in poetic ontology? How is an incident different from an event? How does chance determine time? Or perhaps chance has nothing to do with time? The poetics of Oberiu juxtaposes theories of predictable, 'designed' work and the metaphysics of chance, the interpretation of the 'true' causes and purposes of a creative act and the ability

---

1   Vladimir Dal, *Tolkovyi slovar' zhivogo velikorusskogy yazyka* [Explanatory dictionary of the living Great Russian language], Volume 4, Moscow, 1955, 226.

2   As will become clear from the context, the Russian word *'sluchai'* used here is difficult to render into English consistently while maintaining the same effect: *sluchai* means *chance* (as something that happens randomly and unpredictably) but also a *case*, a *happening*, an *occurrence*, an *accident* or an *incident* (as in a traffic accident, a story, a particular event – 'let me tell you about a thing that happened'). When referring to an abstract notion of unpredictability and randomness, we use 'chance'. In all other cases, we use an appropriate term and, if necessary, insert an explanation to provide additional context. – *Trans.*

to make use of a favourable opportunity. That is what Vvedensky understood by the poetic critique of reason, and he was not the only one. Other
members of the group shared this view. Druskin dwelled on the notion of
the ontological status of 'randomness' for many years (we may recall his
studies of dodecaphony in Schoenberg, Alban Berg, Anton von Webern,
and his readings of Meister Eckhart and Søren Kierkegaard). Many of his
reflections revolved around the explanation of the origin of the creative
act – was it characterised by randomness or was it based on a perfectly
rational choice and the predictability of subsequent steps? The likes of
Edgar Poe, Mallarmé and Paul Valery insisted on eliminating any sign of
randomness from a literary work (although it is difficult to say that Mallarmé attained the clarity of thought he needed to justify his own choice:
the idea of the perfect Book).[3]

There are several strategies here: one interprets chance as *fate*; another
as an *incident*; the third as a *miracle*; the fourth as an *event*. We often
hear the following at the beginning of a story or an anecdote: 'And here's
another thing that happened . . .' We usually say: 'but he was lucky, he
was born under a lucky star', 'he always gets lucky'. An incident is often
correlated not with an event, but with fate; in an existential time, these
two become equal. After all, we do say: 'What an interesting incident!'
An incident or a story of one's life as a chain of symptoms, an order of the
random before an experience of an event series.[4]

---

3   See, for example, the following observations by Druskin: 'Tachisme is the identity
of the *random* and the regular. It is found in any act of creativity, and it was previously
called inspiration. But now it is done consciously. Dodecaphony provides a method for
the *identity* of the random and the regular: the basic image represents *millions* of possibilities or chances, it does not exclude inspiration, since it is impossible to go through all of
these chances, but it allows inspiration to take its course while in the past inspiration was
almost completely arbitrary. But, even putting it this way is not quite correct; previously
inspiration used to be more constrained – by harmony, by classical counterpoint – while
now it is free and at the same time it also receives direction . . . In creativity of a high
style, I abandon myself and dedicate myself to the object of art. There is a subjective
randomness here – I suddenly find something new in the object, but for the object itself
it is something regular; but there is also an absolute randomness in the object, perhaps
it is something incomprehensible in a poem, without which the poem is bad (according
to Goethe). But complete Tachisme either destroys the regularity in the object itself, or
severely reduces it. See, for example, Stockhausen. In absolute randomness, the object
exists only for an instant' (Druskin, *Dnevniki, 1963–1979*, 2001, 459–60). ('Tachisme' is
a technique of managing 'randomness'. Druskin was familiar with the works of Stockhausen, Boulez and other avant-garde composers.)

4   In the traditional American biography genre, there is a concept of a *case-history*.

If we abandon the Greek idea of cyclical time and eternal periodic-
ity, we would probably be more intensely conscious of the exceptional
nature of an *opportunity*. An opportunity is fundamentally tragic,
and rhetoric skilfully deploys its pathos. In time that is irreversible,
an opportunity is 'unique', 'without precedent and unrepeatable'. It is
neither predictable nor does it ever recur. We can neither prepare for
it in advance nor recoup it afterward. It is always a first (and last time),
always 'impromptu'.[5]

Let us add that it is impossible to interpret an opportunity [*sluchai*],
because unlike an event that demands the presence of an observer, an
opportunity has a pure singular form, it cannot be interpreted differently
than what it is – an instantly passing phenomenon of life. There are many
opportunities, but none of them has yet been repeated, which means
that an opportunity is part of our inalienable experience. As we can see,
whatever inadvertently and unexpectedly happens to us, to others, to the
world in general, happens by chance. But chance confirms the unpredictability of each instant. Life is an unorganised and unanticipated chain of
random occurrences. But what about our plans, our will and our aspiration to reach a goal (to be successful)? Are we not trying to manage the
randomness of life? Unfortunately, this is not a convincing argument, for
what matters is not what a person regards as his achievement today, but
how it came to be realised in a random fashion. Chance is of the order
of *consequences*; event is of the order of *causes*. But consequences cannot
explain causes, just as we cannot explain why the same causes produce
different consequences. Just to clarify – what appears under the guise of
chance has its own secret name, and this name is *truth*, a truth that we
cannot change.

So, what is the relationship between *chance* and time?

Can we begin by looking at a general or objective time, time that
changes everything, that 'passes', 'runs', of which we have either 'not

---

Psychoanalysis can be considered as a biography of *a case*, including from the instrumental side of things. The opposition of an incident and an event is resolved in the course of
the psychoanalytical session: becoming an event in a patient's history, an incident loses
its clinical acuity and intrusiveness, it is neutralised.

5   François Jullien, *A Treatise on Efficacy: Between Western and Chinese Thinking*, trans. Janet Lloyd, Honolulu: University of Hawaii Press, 2004, 77. (In the Russian
translation of this book, cited by Podoroga, the word *sluchai* is used whenever we see
'opportunity' in this citation. – *Trans.*)

enough' or 'too much', or, in relation to which, we have 'a lot of time to spare'? This time, if we take a closer look at it, is divided into what *was*, what *is* and what *will be*; it is objective time, the time of numerical correlations (measures, dates, divisions, calculations, even though all this remains purely external to the time-experience). Let us suppose that there are two worlds: one immersed in a *lethargic sleep*, and in which time has stopped; and another, waking, 'living', flowing world, where time does not stand, where it flows. One kind of time we will call *large-scale* time (other special kinds of time are included here: physical time, chronographic time, cosmological time and so on); here the course of time makes sense only in terms of its sequence and irreversibility; it is external to us, but also alongside us; it is an objective scale for our calculations, hopes and defeats. This is a finite time for all beings trying to perceive it; in it, there is death and completion of the lifecycle; death as a measurement, a number, a statistic. In this time, there is no present, or, more precisely, it is elusive, because this time is substantive, spatial, it does not tolerate that which is unconditioned and materially unrealised. But there is another kind of time, *small-scale* time, intensive as opposed to extensive and formal time; this is experienced, existential time; it can be impulsive, accelerating, but also extremely slow; it can open up in an intertwining of instants, be dispersed, sparse, almost empty, devoid of air, but also saturated, extremely dense, tense, ready to explode. The defining feature of this time: *it endures, and it does not repeat itself.*

Everything that repeats itself acquires a spatial form, becomes a *habit*. In our calculations, when using objective time, we rely on a habit, because it correlates our own experience of time with time that is independent of us. The habit creates an illusion of our adaptability to the natural time, the cosmic time of Nature. There are zones of interaction between these two types of time. When the large-scale time invades the small-scale time, the result is an Event (often of a catastrophic kind); when the small-scale time invades the large-scale time, we get a Chance. Therefore, chance is related to our evaluation of external time, for which no randomness (no cessation, no rupture, no pause) exists. Randomness introduces small-scale time into the world. Any creative effort requires for itself at least a moment of stopped time, a short interval, at times intensive, at times explosive. A poetic substance is born in these gaps, which tear holes in the passage of objective time in the most unexpected places; it flickers like yellow dots of gold in the dark layers of a rich vein. Where we are subject to the flow of large-scale time, there we are ruled by habits, by the rituals of everyday life. Then, any incident, and indeed any randomness as such, looks like a mistake, like a disregard for the daily pragmatism of life, and sometimes it appears as fate. By making small-scale time inaccessible to large-scale time, we become poets. As we go deeper into small-scale time, we experiment with poetic speech, with dream-like and hallucinogenic practices (drugs), and, of course, with play.

But then one wonders: what does it mean to stop the world's time? Or does it stop by itself? In Perrault's fairy tale the lethargic sleep of the princess does not stop the general time; on the contrary, that time is still passing while bypassing the princess (and her castle with all its inhabitants); her world is enclosed on itself and exists outside of time. In fact, any cessation of the world-time, if it were possible, would lead to a complete disaster, to the end of the world. Chance is the name of the cessation of habit, of that 'frequency and density of what is really happening'. Chance certifies the interruption by connecting interrupted pieces together, it 'patches up' temporal gaps; when nothing happens and there is no reason for something to happen: 'it is no more than a fugitive and fleeting "infinitesimal" point of contact. It flashes by like a streak of lightning, in "next to no time".'[6] But when that which occurs becomes an occurrence, then comes the time to evaluate what has occurred. And out of everything that did occur, something may turn out to be a 'lucky chance' or an 'unlucky' one. After all, for Kharms, Vaginov and Vvedensky, and of course, for Lipavsky, the chief philosopher of Oberiu, the common way to think about it was found in a simple method of *comparing everything with everything* (words, events, things and occurrences, facts and ideas).[7] Vaginov's hero collects tiny pieces of events of post-revolutionary time, which he retains in the form of newspaper cuttings, wrappers, 'fingernails', cigarette butts, pictures; all these absurd strange remnants, mostly garbage, extracted from a single flow of time, form bizarre collections of random, useless and spent being. In Oberiu, the (Aristotelian) aesthetics of pure repetition falls apart, and the metaphysics of Chance comes to the fore.

---

6   Ibid., 77.

7   Konstantin Vaginov, *Polnoe sobranie sochinenii v proze* [A complete collection of prose works], St Petersburg, 1999, 79.

The World's Humour, or *the Falsification of Incidence*

Daniil Kharms was the virtuoso of the technique of *incidence*.[8] True, in Kharms it does not have the meaning of some wonderful, incredible thing that can happen to everyone, that can interrupt the boredom of life. Kharms actually contrasts an incident with a *miracle*: one expects a miracle, but it is not possible, while an incident is not expected, but is possible (and it kills faith in miracles). One set of his texts Kharms called 'incidences'. Describing incidents is the only complete form of the literary record. A lack of understanding of what happened as an intrigue. A minimalist style is chosen, and that only reinforces the effect of an almost biblical simplicity of utterance, at times to the point of absurdity. An utterance appears to be largely meaningless precisely because of the oversimplicity, brevity and monotony of what is happening. Everything is immediately immersed in the boredom of repetition. To use chance as seems appropriate; as a result, every incident is presented in the form of a random occurrence, not as an event. An incident cannot become an event. There is no need to look for a deeper understanding of the causes of what happened, because these causes have no meaning.

At first glance, Kharms' theory of incidence is close to the Dadaist tradition (and not to surrealism). Above all, because Oberiu's 'incidents' contain nothing miraculous, but plenty that is curious, mocking, satirically grotesque, incredible, that becomes a comical gesture, which does not need any interpretation. Kharms' incidents are not about what happened, but about what happens all the time and what is difficult to call an incident. There is something grotesque about it; there is a skilful 'perversity' in the play of mind: I would call it a *falsification* of incidence. Indeed, for Kharms an incident is a short story, extremely concise in terms of length, and minimalist in style; and it is not even a 'short story', but a light weapon of war used to attack a traditional literary form such as a 'long-form story' (a novella, a novel, or a long poem) that has a plot line, characters, an end and a beginning. Kharms understood his own technique very well, and even taught others how to write 'incidents'. Thus, he distinguished between three different types of incidents: an 'explanation',

---

8   Neil Cornwell translated Kharms' book *Sluchai* as 'Incidences'. See Daniil Kharms, *Incidences*, trans. Neil Cornwell, London: Serpent's Tail, 1994. We use 'incidence' or 'incident' in the context of that text and related texts; otherwise, we follow the strategy of translating *sluchai* outlined above. – *Trans.*

a 'description' and, finally, what he called a 'demonstrated phenomenon'. Here is what he wrote about this: 'A phenomenon of this sort, despite its abstractness and semantic remoteness, must be taken literally. Any action described in this way attains the maximum specificity. Description ceases to be description and becomes the action itself, to which one may attach a unitary label. Hence also the name of the device: "Labelled action" (which is the same as a demonstrated action).'[9] In sum, an incident is distinguished by *demonstrativeness*; Kharms rejects a rhetoric of image, rejects all representation; an incident must shock us with its literalness; in other words, it must have a performative effect.

Even if we take longer texts by Kharms (it does not matter if they are poetry, prose or plays), we can see that they are all made up of the same smaller forms – of 'incidents'. Moreover, there is no particular sequence when it comes to the plot; everything is added haphazardly, without any explanation and *randomly*, as if it had just occurred to the author (and he was too lazy to cross it out). What is being demonstrated by this? For example, characters *A* and *B* produce a comic effect while they are swapping places, repeating one another, as long as actions that violate behavioural norms are imposed on them. First, we see a sort of *rocking* motion; it resembles a dance, and it comes before the start of a *rotation*. Various pieces join the action: *this* one and *that* one, *this* and *that*. There is no dialectics here, only perhaps a purely musical form of repetition. Each 'incident' deals with a finite nothing; it ends with the complete disintegration of the hero or his environment, and this attraction to 'destruction' determines the continuity of repetition, rocking, which ultimately becomes what Lipavsky called *reverse rotation* (not necessarily just in a counterclockwise direction). Each incident has one obsessive theme, expressed in one verb form (for example, *to lie down, to sleep, to fall out/ to fall down, to hit in the face, to fly, to die, to not be, to not have* and so on). This, however, does not mean that the entire action is necessarily built around one verb; often in more complex 'incidents' it is interrupted by the intrusion of another, no less random factor. The monotony of a story-incident, its predictability, is violated by the discrepancy between the subject's action and the verb form used in connection with it. The beginning of each 'incident' is as random as its end.

---

9   Daniil Kharms, *'I Am a Phenomenon Quite Out of the Ordinary': The Notebooks, Diaries, and Letters of Daniil Kharms*, ed. Anthony Anemone and Peter Scotto, Boston: Academic Studies Press, 2013, 139–40.

Here are some examples of Kharms' 'incidents':

There was once a redheaded man, who had no eyes or ears. He had no hair either, so people called him redheaded only in a manner of speaking. He couldn't speak, since he had no mouth. He also had no nose. He didn't even have arms or legs. And he didn't have a stomach, and he didn't have a back, and he didn't have a spine, and he didn't have any insides. He had nothing. So it's impossible to understand what we're talking about. Far better if we talk about him no longer.[10]

The Plummeting Old Women

A certain old woman, out of excessive curiosity, fell out of a window, plummeted to the ground, and was smashed to pieces. Another old woman leaned out of the window and began looking at the remains of the first one, but she also, out of excessive curiosity, fell out of the window, plummeted to the ground and was smashed to pieces. Then a third old woman plummeted from the window, then a fourth, then a fifth. By the time a sixth old woman had plummeted down, I was fed up watching them, and went off to Mal'tseviskiy Market where, it was said, a knitted shawl had been given to a certain blind woman.[11]

Incidents

One day, Orlov stuffed himself with mashed peas and died. And Krylov, on finding out about this, also died. And Spiridonov died of his own accord. And Spiridonov's wife fell off the sideboard and also died. And Spiridonov's children drowned in the pond. And Spiridonov's grandmother hit the bottle and took to the road. And Mikhailovich stopped combing his hair and went down with mange. And Kruglov sketched a woman with a whip in her hands and went out of his mind. And Perekhrestov received four hundred roubles by wire and put on such airs that he got chucked out of work. They are good people all – but they can't keep their feet firmly on the ground.[12]

---

10   Ibid., 478.
11   Kharms, *Incidences*, 50.
12   Ibid., 49.

An Encounter

On one occasion a man went off to work and on the way he met another man who, having bought a loaf of Polish bread, was wending his way home.

And that's just about all there is to it.[13]

Mashkin Killed Koshkin

Comrade Koshkin danced around Comrade Mashkin.

Comrade Mashkin followed Comrade Koshkin with his eyes.

Comrade Koshkin insultingly waved his arms and repulsively shook his legs.

Comrade Mashkin put on a frown.

Comrade Koshkin twitched his belly and stamped his right foot.

Comrade Mashkin let out a cry and flung himself at Comrade Koshkin.

Comrade Koshkin tried to run away, but stumbled and was overtaken by Comrade Mashkin.

Comrade Mashkin struck Comrade Koshkin on the head with his fist.

Comrade Koshkin let out a cry and fell to his hands and knees.

Comrade Mashkin put the boot in to Comrade Koshkin under the belly and once more struck his across the skull with his fist.

Comrade Koshkin measured his length on the floor and died.

Mashkin killed Koshkin.[14]

Fight Story

Alexey Alexeyevich squashed Andrei Karlovich beneath him and, having pummelled his face, let him go.

Andrei Karlovich turned pale with rage, threw himself at Alexey Alexeyevich, and hit him in the teeth.

Alexey Alexeyevich, surprised by such a quick attack, fell on the floor. Then Andrei Karlovich straddled him, took his dentures out of his mouth and so thoroughly worked over Alexey Alexeyevich with them that the latter rose from the floor with a mutilated face and a torn nostril. With his hands over his face, Alexei Alexeyevich ran away.

---

13   Ibid., 67.
14   Ibid., 72.

Meanwhile, Andrei Karlovich wiped down his dentures, inserted them into his mouth, clicked his teeth together, looked around and, catching no glimpse of Alexei Alexeyevich, went looking for him.[15]

The Dream

Kalugin fell asleep and had a dream that he was sitting in some bushes and a policeman was walking past the bushes.

Kalugin woke up, scratched his mouth and went to sleep again and had another dream that he was walking past some bushes and that a policeman had hidden in the bushes and was sitting there.

Kalugin woke up, put a newspaper under his head, so as not to wet the pillow from his dribblings, and went to sleep again; and again he had a dream that he was sitting in some bushes and a policeman was walking past the bushes.

Kalugin woke up, changed the newspaper, lay down and went to sleep again. He fell asleep and had another dream that he was walking past some bushes and a policeman was sitting in the bushes.

At this point Kalugin woke up and decided not to sleep any more, but he immediately fell asleep and had a dream that he was sitting behind a policeman and some bushes were walking past.

Kalugin let out a yell and tossed about in bed but couldn't wake up.

Kalugin slept straight through for four days and four nights and on the fifth day he awoke so emaciated that he had to tie his boots to his feet with string, so that they didn't fall off. In the bakery where Kalugin always bought wheaten bread, they didn't recognize him and handed him a half-rye loaf.

And a sanitary commission which was going round the apartments, on catching sight of Kalugin, decided that he was insanitary and no use for anything and instructed the janitors to throw Kalugin out with the rubbish.

Kalugin was folded in two and thrown out as rubbish.[16]

Let us take a closer look at these examples. Is there not an obvious gap between our own corporeal habit, which allows us to gain new experiences without rejecting the previously acquired ones, and the interactions

---

15   Daniil Kharms, *Today I Wrote Nothing: The Selected Writings of Daniil Kharms,* trans. Matvei Yankelevich, New York: The Overlook Press, 2007, 57.

16   Kharms, *Incidences,* 58–9.

of bodies that we encounter when we look at Kharms' 'incidents'? Complete conversion of the subject, violation of manageability: the verb takes over the position of the subject, turning the latter into an appendage of action, which leads to a loss of meaning, since the subject means nothing in and of itself. In standard grammar the subject does not lose its main functions; in fact, they are often emphasised. Here, however, there is a ban on any natural – *mimetic* – response that would point the reader in the direction of real events and facts that must somehow correlate with the story. As a result, there is a strong comic effect. What we see before us are empty signs, hieroglyphs and ciphers, even the names of characters mean nothing. There is no room for referential illusion. Its lack is compensated with a wave of laughter; the comedy is the only reality that the poet is taking into consideration. The language is bloodless; it loses its living flesh; the phrases are abstract, flat, and express nothing but naked activity; but this is only true until some juxtaposition causes shock, or a temporary misunderstanding, which is then reinforced in the presentation of 'what actually happened'. The incident is part of a comic demonstration of reality, it is precisely humour that gives us back a sense of reality. Nonsense acquires meaning as soon as the play of laughter begins. That is why, in Kharms, nonsense makes sense, why humour incredibly convincingly falsifies any explanation of what happened.

Laughter is our reaction to the gesticulation of someone who suddenly falls for no apparent reason. What then is the gesture of Oberiu? I think this gesture has three components: *abyss, emptiness* and *Nothing*.

In the *Duino Elegies* Rilke refers to the 'circumspection of a human gesture' as having an inner limit that prevents it from becoming violent, too obvious, unguarded.

> Didn't the caution of human gestures on Attic steles
> amaze you? Weren't love and separation placed
> on those shoulders so lightly they seemed made
> of other stuff than we are? Remember the hands:
> despite the power in the torso, they lie weightless.
> The self-controlled knew this: we can only go this far.
> All we can do is touch one another like this.[17]

---

17   Rainer Maria Rilke, *Duino Elegies and The Sonnets of Orpheus*, trans. A. Poulin, Jr. Boston: Houghton Mifflin Company, 1977, 17.

Thus, in my opinion, the gesture of Oberiu is imprudent, transgressive, without an awareness of inner measure. It is directed at objects, bodies and events, and it is never returned. The curve of the unreturned gesture. A gesture that belongs to no one or a transcendental gesture? After the gesture invades the language-world, the language separates itself from the world, and the world changes its face; it is no longer the same world. In it, there is no language guarded by our gestures. Therefore, the gesture of Oberiu is always destructive, though I cannot say it is violent. Perhaps the collection of individual poetic gestures of each of the members of Oberiu would be quite rich. We learn about them in autobiographical notes, new legends, rumours, memories of friends, partners and contemporaries. The poetic worlds of Vvedensky and Kharms can only exist as long as their 'imprudent gesture' is repeated. The physical energy of the gesture is impressive, it attracts us from the first moments of reading, and it is perhaps the only thing we enjoy so fully. The gesture of Oberiu controls the logic of repeating the same action for different objects. The object is extracted from its everyday environment and immediately loses its usual qualities and forms of existence. We acquire the meaning of the event not from a set of particularly positioned objects, but from the event itself, which is by its nature pre-substantive and located in the realm of the pre-meaning.

The gesture produced by Oberiu's poetic energy is an event in which everyday things acquire new modes of existence. Old women fall and plummet all the time, precisely because they are dead, and they are dead because they constantly fall, rise back to their feet only to fall again . . . The gesture of a forced-but-free fall ('collapse') is elaborated in the chain of repetitions of a single event. The gesture of Oberiu 'endures', it cannot be completed, so it repeats itself again and again, giving objects and bodies the chance to get rid of their former properties. These gestures are never lacking, there must always be too many of them, they are 'incidents': gestures of a scuffle, eating, coitus, cutting off organs and stitching them back on, gestures of bodies that are walking, standing, sitting, crawling, lying, flying, rising, falling . . .

Once upon a time, a fly collided with the forehead of a gentleman running by and, passing through his head, exited out the back.[18]

And the wind, blowing into the hillside, passed right through it, not even throwing it off its path. It was as though this hill of chartaceous origin had lost its property of impermeability. For example, a gull had transected the hill in its flight. It went right through it as though through a cloud. This observation was confirmed by several witnesses.[19]

All of a sudden, a fly zoomed out of the house, buzzed around and around, and slammed into the igumen's forehead. It slammed into his forehead, flew through his head, and exiting out the back, flew back into the house.[20]

If we read these transparent and childishly pure texts carefully, we should not limit ourselves to the tasks of a philologist-practitioner or a psychiatrist-theorist, who would create a list of similar gestures-events. It can be said that practically any work in the archive of Oberiu, especially a small one, is capable of expressing its own gesture inherent in the entirety of its boredom and monstrosity of non-accomplishment, of actively expressing the absence of any action. The gesture of Oberiu is a source of meaninglessness; it is valuable in and of itself; it is already an event and therefore it does not need to be interpreted ('to make sense'); it is meant for nothing, it is simply the discovery of new possibilities of existence of objects and bodies, mired in a boredom of time and therefore immovable and dead.

The order of the kinetic organisation of an 'incident' can be different: *a chain* (a relay) of repeated actions; *a splitting*, or an exhaustion of the properties of an object, an event, a corporeal image; *a double game* of this-or-that (a kind of exchange between *this* and *that*). The incident draws many nonreal and made-up random accidents into its ironic play. In my opinion, Kharms as a comedian is closest to Buster Keaton. Behind

18   Daniil Kharms, 'The Family Gibberundum', in *Russian Absurd: Selected Writings*, trans. Alex Cigale, Evanston, IL: Northwestern University Press, 2017, 10.

19   Ibid., 12.

20   Ibid., 13.

the absurdity and the meaninglessness of his 'incidents', we must see a
laughter-related comic motivation: we are made to laugh, we are forced
to laugh at nonsense, thus neutralising its dramatic impact. Kharms'
techniques are close to Buster Keaton's so-called 'gags'. What's a *gag*? It
is a character's action that leads to a collision with the outside world. A
gag is an element of a comic situation, it is absurd, because it exists on
its own, independent of a situation in which it *suddenly* manifests itself:
'if the gag opens out on absurd discourse, it never does so in a gratuitous
manner, that is to say, never independently of the disturbed realistic discourse. It is precisely by overstepping the norms of the realistic story that
the gag makes those realistic norms apparent.'[21] A gag is an ostensibly
destructive and violent tool invented by the silent cinema for a comic
refutation of behavioural norms. Like gags, Kharms' set of gestures in his
'incidents' is unmotivated and at the same time absolutely random, his
comedy is intrusive. A gag is a sudden short-circuiting of the opposites
that creates a spark; this is what causes a spasm of laughter. This is the
laughter mechanism in Keaton's gags: it is the circuit of action that would
be impermissible and extremely dangerous for the hero in real life. It is
so easy to break the orderly routine of daily life; one only requires two
or three 'precise' hits of a gag. Randomness enters life by means of a gag;
one of the aims of this operation is to represent the world as being much
less secure than it appears. Gags are the response of an 'insignificant
man' to the dangerous technical environment that surrounds him. The
kinetic energy of Kharms' 'incidents' is sapped by repetition and the
absurdity of what is happening, yet it is present in each of them quite
clearly; something always happens while not happening. The incident
never took place after all; but that does not mean it did not happen. Any
action is a chain or an entire cluster of actions, where everything that is
predictable is actively eroding the conventional standard of behaviour.
The incident is blocked by nonsense. Kharms' every incident is a collection of depictions of the nonsensical. It can be said that the genuine
incident is the opposite of nonsense, for it happens, i.e. it has a beginning
and an end in time.

---

21   Sylvain Du Pasquier and Norman Silverstein, 'Buster Keaton's Gags', *Journal of
Modern Literature* 3:2 (April 1973), 276 [269–1].

The Principle: 'Some equilibrium with a small deviation'

What is *a small deviation*? It is that which disturbs the equilibrium of the system while simultaneously supporting its development (its vitality).[22] This principle was invented by Druskin in 1933.[23] In the realms of experience where his thought moves, a thought that is disciplined and trained in the logic of the argument, there emerge themes that illustrate the relationship of the principle of 'a small deviation' and the dynamic aspects of the system's existence as a whole (poetic, philosophical, and any other system). In other words, the system's equilibrium is achieved through *a small* disturbance that allows the equilibrium to acquire a new quality of stability; using contemporary language to describe this, we can say that chaos opens up the possibility of order. A small deviation is a particular incident that became a hieroglyph of change. Here are Druskin's typical reflections on the subject:

> Some equilibrium with a small deviation is a disturbance and restoration of equilibrium. *This disturbance and restoration exist now and now, always now.* But when the equilibrium is restored, it is indeterminate by the second kind of indeterminacy. The disturbance and restoration are just a way to understand some equilibrium with a small deviation, we notice it only when it was just disturbed or just restored.[24]

---

22 There are direct parallels with the problem of entropy here. Every organism seeks to keep itself from moving to a state of 'equilibrium'. The thermodynamic state of equilibrium is a state of *maximum entropy*: 'Every process, event, happening – call it what you will; in a word, everything that is going on in Nature means an increase of the entropy of the part of the world where it is going on. Thus, a living organism continually increases its entropy – or, as you may say, produces positive entropy – and thus tends to approach the dangerous state of maximum entropy, which is death. It can only keep aloof from it, i.e. alive, by continually drawing from its environment negative entropy – which is something very positive as we shall immediately see. What an organism feeds upon is negative entropy. Or, to put it less paradoxically, the essential thing in metabolism is that the organism succeeds in freeing itself from all the entropy it cannot help producing while alive' (Erwin Schrödinger, *What Is Life? The Physical Aspect of the Living Cell*, Cambridge: Cambridge University Press, 1967, 71).

23 'In 1933, I found a term: "some equilibrium with a small deviation". I've been looking for it for something like six years. I felt its religious significance then, and it became completely clear to me later' (Yakov Druskin, *Dnevniki, 1928–1962* [Diaries, 1928–1962], St Petersburg, 2001, 532).

24 Ibid., 69.

Some equilibrium does not take place and does not have an origin; it cannot be disturbed and cannot be restored. Some equilibrium with a small deviation exists in the visible, in that which is taking place; equilibrium's small deviation is the visibility of origin and time, but the equilibrium itself is not in time. I notice it as a disturbance and restoration, I notice the small deviation. Equilibrium is revealed to me in disturbance; but when it is restored, it is restored only in the visible, because equilibrium itself is not disturbed and restored but simply is; then I see nothing. I observe restoration of equilibrium as an empty, unfilled time without events. This time does not move, does not pass, it simply is. But the equilibrium also does not have an origin, it is not disturbed or restored, but simply is. Time is a form of a certain restored equilibrium with a small deviation. It is a time of emptiness and boredom. Another kind of time – time of events – is a small deviation in some equilibrium.

What interests me now in time? If I say that time is a form of a certain equilibrium that has just been restored, it should be understood as follows: if time does not exist, if time is only an illusion, then I perceive time in some equilibrium when this equilibrium is being restored. Thus, the time of emptiness and boredom is a form of a small deviation in some equilibrium when this equilibrium is being restored. But now I am interested in something else: if time does not exist, then there is no change. I imagine eternity as an instant, and what was before that instant no longer exists; this is related to states or possibilities of an instant. But I find nothing beneficial for myself in an instant. In an instant I find something alien. It scares me, and I want to have another eternity to give me comfort; eternity is connected with the idea of reward, and therefore the idea of the future, i.e. time is reintroduced. But this is incorrect.[25]

A perfect system – a perfect threshold – is death. A history of a small deviation: initially, a deviation was only a deviation, an unavoidable flaw. But then I saw that a system without a deviation contained an even greater deviation, a deviation of a threshold. Then a deviation became an advantage. But it stopped being a deviation. Misunderstanding, puzzlement, 'pain of existence' cannot be excluded from the deviation,

---

25   Ibid., 71.

as D.I. [Kharms] and I wanted to do: a certain amount of misunderstanding is understanding.[26]

Let us try to explain these passages. We can take, for example, a
kaleidoscope: as soon as one turns the tube, the picture changes, seemingly randomly but with an expected result. The configuration of the
next image depends on the nature of the original operations ('a limited
number of patterns'). Randomness hides in the smallest deviations that
cannot be detected, where randomness is not controlled or designed. In
a fully random kaleidoscope, each turn would create a new pattern, and
none of the patterns could ever be repeated. The most inconspicuous
and insignificant changes would produce the largest consequences, as
Nietzsche said: 'Thoughts that come on the feet of doves steer the world.'[27]
This is a randomness of another sort that is present in any, even the most
automated and 'strict' system; it could be a jump, a flash, a transition or a
barely noticeable shift. Macro-randomness can be accounted for, micro-
randomness cannot. The ancient Greek philosopher Epicurus reflected
on the beginning of the world precisely from the point of view of 'a small
deviation' and gave it a name: *clinamen*. In his poetic cosmogony *On
the Nature of Things*, Lucretius described this kind of initial *deviation*
perfectly and in some detail. The world, according to Epicurus, consists
of matter and void (emptiness), the particles of matter fall in an infinite,
unending space. Thus, a conclusion: if the atoms of matter were falling
without touching one another, without deviating, the world would not
have begun. Therefore, at the world's origin, there is always 'a small deviation'. The slightest, minor disturbance, the almost intangible collision of
one atom with another, causes the uncontrolled chain reaction of other
deviations. But, most importantly, the notion of the clinamen points to
the freedom and autonomy of atoms; otherwise, they would have clung
together and formed a lump.[28] But because atoms are eternal units, resil-
ient, like firmly inflated rubber balls, and they come in countless numbers,

---

26   Ibid., 212.

27   Cf. Friedrich Nietzsche, *Thus Spoke Zarathustra*, trans. Adrian del Caro, Cambridge: Cambridge University Press, 2006, 117.

28   For example, Michel Serres believes that this is precisely why the world of
ancient Greeks looks so calm and harmonious – they made a pact with things. Things,
like people, obey the gods. Cf. Michel Serres, *The Birth of Physics*, trans. Jack Hawkes,
Manchester: Clinamen Press, 2000. See also Ilya Prigogine and Isabelle Stengers, *Order
Out of Chaos: Man's New Dialogues with Nature*, London: Verso Books, 2018, 303–4;

they collide and fly apart as a result of their own collisions, forming entire settlements of matter (water, land, fire, sky, human bodies and so on).

> And the atoms move continuously for all time, some recoiling far apart from one another [upon collision], and others, by contrast, maintaining a [constant] vibration when they are locked into a compound or enclosed by the surrounding [atoms of a compound]. This is the result of the nature of the void which separates each of them and is not able to provide any resistance; and their actual solidity causes their rebound vibration to extend, during the collision, as far as the distance which the entanglement [of the compound] permits after the collision. There is no principle for these [entities], since the atoms and the void are eternal.[29]

Consequently, no matter how high the frequency of collisions experienced by a single atom-ball, there still exists a moment of freedom for each. And that means that, at every moment, a great incident renews the world. And it relies on the existence of a global void: not a separated void, but an all-penetrating void that joins and disjoins everything. What we have here is a play of void. No feature of the cosmos can be explained without this void that is as eternal as the matter in which this void exists.[30] Of course, it is risky to link Epicurus' cosmogonic views and the poetic ontology of the members of Oberiu, yet the image of the *clinamen* may be a good test of their notion of 'a small deviation'.

Gilles Deleuze, *The Logic of Sense*, trans. Mark Lester with Charles Stivale, London: The Athlone Press, 1990, 266–79.

29   Epicurus, *The Epicurus Reader: Selected Writings and Testimonia*, trans. Brad Inwood and L.P. Gerson, Indianapolis: Hackett Publishing Company, 1994, 7–8.

30   In his reflections on the atoms of Epicurus and the *clinamen*, Derrida drew attention to the etymology of the French terms 'chance' and 'cas', which, in addition to their main dictionary meaning, also mean to *fall* (to *fall down*), and this resonates with a series of other lexical groups ('cadence', 'choir', 'echeoir', 'echeance', 'accident', 'incident') that go back to the Latin *cadere*. In the German language, *Zufall* or *Zufalligkeit*, as Derrida puts it, designate a 'chance': 'for *zufallen* (to fall due), *zufällig*, the accidental, fortuitous, contingent, occasional – and the word "occasion" belongs to the same Latin descent. A *Fall* is a case; *Einfall*, an idea that suddenly comes to mind in an apparently unforeseeable manner. Now, I would say that the unforeseeable is precisely the case, involving as it does that which falls and is not seen in advance' (Jacques Derrida, 'My Chances/Mes Chances: A Rendezvous with Some Epicurean Stereophonies', in *Taking Chances: Derrida, Psychoanalysis*, and Literature, ed. Joseph H. Smith and William Kerrigan, Baltimore: The Johns Hopkins University Press, 1984, 5).

All bodies and souls are made of parts, limited outside and inside by the void that separates and connects. 'A small deviation, if interpreted *naturalistically*, according to Epicurus, represents an infinitely disappearing distance between two atoms (or particles): it is a coupling of a larger or a smaller force, a coupling that is penetrating or gliding, altering or reinforcing, but the force of interaction changes *by chance*, not by necessity. So, how do bodies form? By falling. But this fall is a deviation, for no atom, having started to fall, falls directly downward. And before the atom's fall (the birth of the World), nothing falls at all. In order to introduce an infinite variety of things and events into the world, it is sufficient to create a minimal deviation, i.e. to introduce that 'small deviation' that disrupts the usual course of things. The physically represented 'small deviation' is a *crack*, a *gap*, a *rupture*; it is a force that opens up the space of the void in the dynamic picture of the fall-of-the-world. Essentially, the clinamen or the world deviation is a hypothesis that, on the one hand, allows one to get rid of the void, because the matter reaches maximum density, since it forms everything that exists, but, on the other hand, the world would not exist if it did not fall apart again and again, and that is the consequence of the void. The clinamen connects the void and the matter.

Many members of Oberiu showed an interest in the problem of 'a small deviation', but, first and foremost, it was Lipavsky, Vvedensky and especially Kharms, who even drew sketches of architectural symmetry with a small, barely noticeable imprecision. Kharms' schemes-drawings, illustrating the principle of 'a small deviation', are reproduced here.[31]

Now-time

Previously we saw that *chance*, interpreted by Druskin as 'a small deviation', designates the beginning of everything. It is an unpredictable and mysterious source of life; a pure form of chance as an indicator of the state of any living system that finds equilibrium for an instant that delays the emergence of the random. But what is chance if it is transferred into a temporal system of coordinates? Or, to put it differently: does chance have limits in time? For Druskin, *chance* is not what will happen *tomorrow*, or what happened *yesterday*, but only what is happening *now*.

---

31   Yuri Alexandrov, *Risunki Kharmsa* [Kharms' drawings], St Petersburg, 2006, 34–7.

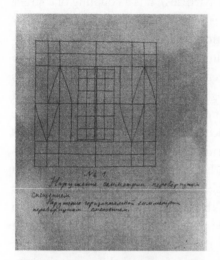

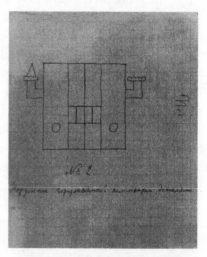

Kharms' drawings of deviations from symmetry

Wherever chance shows itself, that is where the *present* is, and the present is always *now*. Not tomorrow or today, not in an hour, not in a minute, not in an instant. *Now* means *now*. And that means that *now* is an end of something, and not at all a fluid substance of time. If I say that I will do it *now*, then I will do it now. That is why every *now* is performative, and every now is followed by a completed action. When asked *when*, we answer – *now*, or *this* instant. In other words, despite having ended in specific instances, now nonetheless continues to endure. We endure in this *now*, until we tell ourselves: *now* I will do it, I will remember, I will say, I will go, and so on. That is why *now* is the territory of chance. As soon as our ability to act, our reaction to instants of life, weakens, the time of the present, *now-time*, begins to slow down, which leads to a cessation of all time. Every instant turns out to be a new 'small deviation', attacking the general equilibrium of life. There is a curious description of such a 'slowdown' in Druskin's *Diaries*:

> When someone dies slowly and is sick for a long time, this is what is scary: every day, the amount of deterioration is small, so it even seems that the person might be getting better; but suddenly you remember: a week ago, he could lift himself up, and now, he can only roll on his side. But then you forget that observation, and after a while you notice with horror that the person cannot even do that and can only raise his head. And it is the first time you see the inevitability.
>
> So is the end of the world.
>
> Maybe it will be approaching for a year and then arrive in hot weather: it would start in July of one year and end in July of the next year. It would start, maybe like this: from my window or on the street, I would see a man who is no different than any other man except for his walk. He walks a little slower and with more concentration than others. One always notices such people, but then immediately forgets them. That would be the case here as well. Others would see him and notice him and then forget him immediately, and there would be no miracle, because he would appear in different places at different times. When I would see him the second time, I wouldn't be surprised, maybe I wouldn't even remember seeing him before. But in a few days, I would see him for the third time, and then maybe a thought would pass that I have seen him before, but I would forget him yet again. Such meetings would be repeated for two weeks, from July first to July fifteenth. After

the last meeting, there would be some vague sense of concern, but then the meetings would stop for two weeks. He would be seen again in early August. The first meeting would bring some surprise, and even joy, as it does when something familiar returns, but during the future meetings, anxiety would grow and be close to turning into fear but on August fifteenth the meetings would stop again. There would be a feeling that once you focus on the meetings, they're gone, but just stop thinking about them, they're back. The same would happen with the sense of fear at this time. No one would talk about this man, because such talk would seem silly, as it would be silly to talk about too vague a foreboding and a feeling. But in the expression of their faces, when others would be meeting him while I was there – maybe others would try to avoid him, not touch him, or others would act like those people who are afraid of open spaces – I would suddenly realise that others are concerned about these meetings as well. But no one would talk about it, because it would be silly to ask about something when there is no reason to do so, when one has a feeling of foreboding, but the cause is unknown.

On August fifteenth the meetings would end, and in a few days, everyone would calm down, only some concentration and tension would remain. But in the early days of September, meetings would resume, and fear would emerge when the first meeting would take place. But that would only be an anticipation of the real fear. After a few meetings, somewhere where a lot of people gather, and maybe in every house, someone would accidentally say, recalling an event: it all started when a man who was walking slowly showed up. And that is when fear would come. The man who would say that would stop, and everyone would realise that something terrible and irreparable has happened and that everyone already knows it. But then everyone would return to business as usual, and talking about it would be considered indecent, but the constant fear would not leave.

Then everyone would notice that there were already a lot of people walking around slowly, and it would seem that some of their acquaintances have begun to walk slower, too. Maybe they would notice that trams and trains were going slower and the day was getting longer. It won't be possible to talk about it, but the authorities, wanting to calm down the population, would seemingly accidentally report in the newspapers the speed of trams, trains and airplanes, which would seem to have actually slightly increased; and they would also report astronomical facts to prove that the length of the day has not changed. The time would start slowing down, but no science would be able to confirm it, because the clocks would slow down. Then various signs would appear, but again without any miracle and such that they could not even be taken as signs; for example, water in Neva sometimes falls below the average level, but then it returns to the average level; now, however, it would not return or would return, but a few centimetres below the average. Or in the evening, there would be a heavy snow, and then it would be gone overnight. Everything would be in such a state that even the slightest, even if natural, surprise would be frightening. Spring would come very early and the weather would be good. In March, April and May the sun would be bright, sometimes it would rain, but not for too long, there would be no bad weather days. But everyone would already see that the motion had slowed down, even birds would be flying more slowly, and well being in nature and lack of well being in humans would further increase fear: the inevitability of something coming would be felt stronger. Additionally, the anticipation of a hot sunny day and blue sky would be frightening. Fear would reach such a point that it would no longer be possible to distinguish between something natural and something unnatural. Then, at the beginning of June, in the morning everyone would suddenly see that the sun has increased in size. And all of June would be full of very hot sunny days, and if it would rain, then only so that people do not die before their time. And then in July – everything would end.

A gradual acceleration is terrifying, but so is a slowdown, that is, when something happens over time, and when it happens almost naturally, then it is much more frightening than if it were something unnatural.[32]

We can see how inexplicable anxiety, slowly turning into fear, prepares a complete cessation of the world and time. A small deviation that disturbs the system by making it look for a new equilibrium turns out to have the last and most damaging impact, followed by the threat of a cessation and a disruption of equilibrium. Sounds and noises fall silent; a sense of total desolation and indifference sets in; and now the absence

---

32   Druskin, *Dnevniki, 1928–1962*, 87.

of randomness will be confirmed symptomatically by every bird that falls
out of the sky, by every frozen bystander, by every fossilised plant. Once
the principle of 'a small deviation' ceases to function and the equilibrium
of the world is disrupted, the dead ripple of months and days intensifies –
that is when the dying begins. In fact, it is sufficient to turn to Druskin's
diaries of the period of Leningrad siege ('blockage') to immediately see
in real time a depiction of the deceleration of life, its creep toward death.
And the reason for this, of course, was *hunger*:

> In January [of 1942], a deviation entered the new world. Here we
> have an addition through subtraction: I lost a part of myself and then
> temptation arrived. How did that happen? I saw how human strength
> weakened, how sound grew dull, how light faded, how senses died,
> and how feelings fell away. I saw dead lying on the street, I saw death,
> including my own. I was at the limit; and that is when the tempta-
> tion arrived. Ghosts appeared: ghostly people and ghostly worlds.
> They appeared in reality; swollen or dried up faces – two ways to die
> of hunger; there was greed, loss of sense, morning dusk and human
> shadows. I was an observer of the underworld, and, in the evening's
> semi-darkness, its participant.[33]

When *now* is transposed into the register of the spiritual order, the
lonely Protestant 'I', the attitude toward the cessation of the world is
endowed with an intimate-personal emotional order of experience.
Druskin offers his own schematisation of the existential experience of
now-time.[34]

'Now' is at the centre of all existential relations of a person. It is flanked
by two temporal perceptions: on the side of the past, there is *recollection*,
on the side of the future – *anticipation*. As we move in one direction,
toward the past through memory, we immediately discover *now* in terms
of *actual* and *potential* experience *of the present*; the past, as something
actual, is in fact the present, it is found in every instance of *now*; the past,
as something potential, is the ever present possibility of the recollection
itself; in the end, some of us rely on Providence (trying to see the future
from the point of view of the past), and some remain faithful to the daily
automatism of life, using random recollections to support the unity of

33   Ibid., 536.
34   Cf. Yakov Druskin, *Lestnitsa Iakova* [Jacob's ladder], St Petersburg, 2004, 157.

our own person. If we move in the other direction, toward the realm of *anticipation*, we encounter a *challenge*, because the future is unknown to us; we can express our attitude toward it with feelings of *submission* or *equanimity* (*Gelassenheit*), or, at best, *hope*. The other way leads us to *temptation*: we wish to foresee the future, even to manage it; that is when we become *seduced*. We are aware of this, so we experience *fear*, which is expressed in *impatience* and *boredom*, when we want to bring the *anticipated* closer and to give it a name, or when we realise through the power of *fear* the depth of our *sinfulness*, when we prepare ourselves for *repentance*, when we turn to our *conscience* as our judge. That is why at the centre of *now* is the root of the deep personal memory that is trying to preserve the spiritual equilibrium and continue on living.

Often, a person faces a choice that threatens him with a fall, a split; and life itself becomes an unbearable burden if it were not for God who interrupts the temporal *now* by introducing into it that which is extratemporal, eternal, salvific. Druskin reflects:

> When do I have God? *Now*. In recollection, in thought. If it is not now, it is not God but a concept of God. When is God? Also now. Now, having created *something* from *nothing*, having become possible and thus falling off from Him; and *now*, having eliminated itself, having returned to Him, *now* He is and *now* He created me who becomes himself in my recollections, *not now*, but in a possibility and when I actually return to Him as I am *now*. So, two moments of *now*: *now* of God and *now* of my soul. They must be united in a formula; but what kind of union? Both moments of *now* are one *now*, there cannot be *two moments of now*. The formula must show their identity.[35]

Here, too, is another transition into a different time, a sacral and mystical time, a time of *mystery* where we can no longer enter. This *now* is the key moment of existence of poetic substance (linked with existential time). This is an eternal *now*, instantaneously disappearing, flashing, fluid; it is an extremely short duration of an instant. In this *now*, there is no past and no future, only that which is *now*, only that which endures. Thus, in the topography of time it is a multidimensional *point* that consists of *lines*. When randomness is overcome by its own possibility, it is

---

35   Druskin, *Dnevniki, 1928–1962*, 484. Emphases added.

over, and everything stops: 'What now? After all, when all is said and done, this "now" is not determined by what exists or by anything else, but, conversely, everything is determined by this "now". I say – this exists because it is now. "Now" is the criterion of reality, "a seal of authenticity".[36] Our conclusion: for Druskin, *now* is an empty form of duration; in it, everything endures and has no limit. An *incident* rules over *here*, and 'now' itself is *here* where there is God.

Confutatio, or Approximation of God

During Druskin's latter period, the subject of 'a small deviation' leaves the previously outlined boundaries of meaning and enters a meta-religious problematic. A long preoccupation with the music of Bach led Druskin to unexpected conclusions: he discovered that in certain parts of Bach's work there was something like 'containment', a slowdown in musical movement; and as the musical piece approached the apotheosis, there was a more pronounced feeling of a higher Presence: so the listener was given a sense of Bach's 'feeling of bliss', as if God was drawing closer. This is what Druskin noted down:

> When I was showing [Isai] Braudo my analysis of Bach's first Invention [BWV 772], he interrupted me exactly where I was discussing 'Conf<utatio>' (a-moll) and said: here is where you find God in Bach. That was exactly what my formal structural analysis was about: to find the basic intuition of Bach's music that would explain the formal structure of the thing. The order of analysis: Bach's main idea or intuition – structural analysis – a new, clear understanding of music. Bach's basic idea is religious: SDG [Soli Deo Gloria]. But someone who does not know about it can still vaguely sense it but would understand and feel it more clearly only through structural analysis. So, the practical beginning of analysis is structural analysis. And it is the same with Vvedensky: structural analysis is necessary to understand how the basic intuition – time, death, God (in his own words) – was realised in his texts, then these texts would become not only clearer, but they would be experienced better and deeper.[37]

---

36   Ibid., 481.
37   Druskin, *Dnevniki, 1963–1979,* 442.

It is as if a purely rational procedure, based on the initial intuition of a poetic work, opened up a space that no one could ever occupy except the coming God. The word *confutatio* comes from the verb *confuto*, the primary meaning of which is 'to deter, to stop, to calm down'. Hence: *confutatio* means deterring, cessation of motion and time, in order to hear God. The action of *confutatio* produces the effect of spiritual peace, of merging with Deity, a peculiar state of 'spiritual paradise'. And another continuation of the theme of *confutatio*:

> Perhaps the most interesting thing for me was magic. L[ipavsky] thought my texts were ciphers. In Bach I was interested in the crossing of various lines; for a long time, I thought his music was a problem to be solved. That was what I did in my work on Bach. I am looking for the same thing now in Khlebnikov . . . I've been looking for a hidden meaning in Plato's 'conversations'. And what I did find was the secret life of abstract, almost meaningless words-signs; and now I am finding them again while reading *Phaedo*. The same sort of cipher was the hierography that L[ipavsky] and I were working on, and from which I then created my cipher of signs and L[ipavsky] created his *Theory of Words*. Maybe this magic lies at the foundation of thought. Thought is a miracle: a meaningless sign receives meaning. This is regarding the content. A soul is born in this miracle.[38]

Druskin's reflects on the magic of hieroglyphs: 'All my texts started with the vision of some sort of a hieroglyph.'[39]

How does all this intersect with Mallarmé's symbolic mysticism and the initial plasticity of any image, with his material hieroglyphicity?

> The water for Lipavsky was a sign or, as he used to say, a hieroglyph of the original elements; the collision of individuality with the elements, he wrote, was the source of both horror and pleasure. In this respect, he was close to the mystics and to Bach. For Bach, water was the main of the four traditional elements, I think. In his classification of Bach's motifs [Albert] Schweitzer was starting off with the wrong principle that Bach's music was descriptive, therefore he did not notice that in

---

38 Druskin, *Dnevniki, 1928–1962*, 537.
39 Ibid., 530.

Bach a motif of water and a motif of bliss were one and the same: sea ripple, waves, seasickness, all these were related to the weakening of individuality, its loss in the elements, and, among the mystics – in God. The motif of water/bliss often appears in Bach in parts of music that I called *Confutatio*. There is only one, though quite common, motif of Confutatio; after all, Bach avoids all schematism; I counted about twenty themes of Con<futatio> and their meaning, I think, was almost always the same: *the dissolution of a person in a Deity*. So, such unexpected connections are possible: *Theory of Words* and the hieroglyph of water in Lipavsky and the hieroglyph of water in Bach's music.[40]

The apocalyptic tonality is constantly being injected into the game in order to highlight one aspiration: to justify poetry . . . through faith; the justifications provided by poetry itself are not sufficient. The emphasis on the religious quest of the members of Oberiu, so actively announced, leads to poetry becoming a means of achieving goals that lie beyond its limits. A peculiar poetic *sola fide* of Martin Luther. Here Druskin's philosophy plays the same auxiliary role.

Druskin was a philosopher-mystic: his goal was not truth, but mystery. He turned his philosophising into a daily exercise of trying to master the art of reaching something incomprehensible, something mysterious. That is why (this is my hypothesis) the game of encryption, which was pursued by most members of Oberiu (Kharms, Vvedensky, Lipavsky), was defined for Druskin by the goals of personal salvation. Immersed completely in his own mental issues, he did not notice much else. But the deeper the dive into oneself, the more intensely and intimately was the thinkable experienced. It is surprising that everything in Druskin's *Diaries* was subordinate to this unending repetition of what was already said, and there was no Other. The diaries did not address anyone in particular. Perhaps Druskin's philosophical position was formed on the basis of *negative mimesis* as the only way to protect against a world that was extremely hostile and dangerous. The solution was to hide from the world in a mystery, to encrypt one's feelings so that the Other could not penetrate them. I think that such philosophising was a reagent of deep and permanent experiences of fear. Terror, the death of friends, famine during the Leningrad siege – all this was quite enough to begin to perceive the

---

40   Druskin, *Lestnitsa Iakova*, 712–13.

world in a certain way. There is such a concept in Druskin as *indolence* (*ignavia*); he devotes a lot of pages to it in his diaries; it is a state of solitude and acute depression (when nothing can be done). A particularly strong experience of longing-boredom may have been one of the reasons for the *cessation* of the world-time:

> Razliv. I look at the trees and see a slowed down movement: everything is going to pass and is passing right now. I look at trees, sky, birds, nature: none of this exists, it only passes by. I recollect the city; there intervals seem immobile: there was a house, now it is gone, it was destroyed; in the city there are boundaries, so what is within those boundaries seems to be changeless. Nature has no boundaries, at least they are rare – an eruption of a volcano, a flood, there the change is more obvious. But then I remember the city, where there is bustle and movement, and here there is immobility and immutability: firstly, it is as it was, and if there is any movement, then it is a permanent return to what it was and still is, and, secondly, *now*, some significant instant there – movement, but here, only motionlessness. So, three points of view: 1. There – boundaries, here – continuity, therefore, it is more frightening here: firstly, because here everything is unlimited, and secondly, because any movement is felt stronger. 2. There – a significant instant means bustle, but here movement is eternal cycle. 3. There – a significant instant – bustle and movement, here – peace and motionlessness. And a fourth look: there is neither here nor there, but only *now*.[41]

What we have discussed earlier, calling it a cessation of the world and time, seems to be the opposite of the theme of *confutatio*. A sense of fear grows among the mortals as God is leaving, disappearing from their world; all nature and all that is human is gripped by horror, and it is at this point that the time stops, converging with the original annihilation, with the Nothing so often contemplated by the members of Oberiu.

But this is only an assumption. We are only describing transitions (switches) that allow us to present Druskin's reflections or what can be called *equivalents* (or *auto-tautologies*). In human life, according to Druskin, there are two remainders: one superficial and indeterminate, this is *a particular* incident; but there is another, deep, last remainder

---

41   Druskin, *Dnevniki, 1928–1962*, 355–6.

that cannot be reduced to anything, and this is a completely different understanding of the incident – this incident is God. Lipavsky called such transitions *transformations* (from one level of existence to another); schematically they can be represented as follows:

chance
(*a particular incident*)

   as
   '*a small deviation*'
   as
   now
   as
   suspension (of world-time)
   as
   nonsense
   as
   a miracle

chance = *God*
(*final incident*)

All of these concepts are in a relation of transformation with one another, which means that, for example, 'a small deviation', when it is 'a deviation', is identical with 'now', and when it is 'small', then – with not-now, with something not accomplished, fluid, mobile. When it enters the world, it creates a movement toward equilibrium, thereby for an instant suspending its movement, giving rise to nonsense that, for a true poet, might appear as a hieroglyph of mystery, and from there it is only a step to a miracle. This entire series of transformations will never explain the existence of an incident. There is still some remainder that cannot be transformed. Therefore, we come to a conclusion that an incident that does not fit into any event is *God*.

Le hasard objectif: The Theme of 'Miracle' and 'Lucky Chance' in Surrealism

Let's start with an etymological game. There is a cluster of dictionary meanings that describe the *quality* of a chance occurrence: 'lucky chance', 'favourable occasion', 'unheard-of case', 'wonderful event', but also 'unlucky accident', 'tragic incident' and so on; there are also, for example, such introductory phrases as: 'on one occasion . . .', 'by chance', 'just in case', as well as canons of clinical *case-history*, 'exemplary cases'. In life, everything is a chance occurrence [*sluchai*]; nothing is predictable (from birth to death); life is originally presented as if 'on occasion'. But there is another understanding when a chance occurrence is interpreted as a sign of something that takes place regardless of our willingness to accept it and in this case the chance occurrence in question is objectified as fate or destiny. Now the chance occurrence is no longer an accident, but a conduit of fate; this way a tragic accident (as well as a lucky accident) transforms life into fate. In the surrealist interpretation, a 'chance occurrence' is part of the objective (world): *le hasard objectif.* The word 'objective' indicates that the chance occurrence is not a simulation of anything, but a sign of a coming event for which the artist should always be prepared.[42] The objective chance is determined by the temporal scale: *sign/event*:

> The combination sign/event called 'objective chance' thus decomposes into a sign without signification, chronologically prior, followed by an event called 'random' which sustains a privileged relationship with the prior sign. The event 'gives meaning' to the sign; it responds to certain characteristics evoked by the words or pictorial signs in what they signify as well as in their signifiers. This system in its entirety may be called, as I have proposed elsewhere, an 'event margin'.[43]

And further: 'each "event margin" is qualitatively defined, in the sense that the links woven between the sign and the mark of the later event

---

42 Cf. 'Objective chance is the whole of those phenomena which manifest the invasion of daily life by the marvellous' (Michel Carrouges, *André Breton and the Basic Concepts of Surrealism*, trans. Maura Prendergast, Birmingham: University of Alabama Press, 1974, 180).

43 Jacqueline Chénieux-Gendron, *Surrealism*, New York: Columbia University Press, 1990, 82.

have nothing to do with lineal causality. The causal relationships become "twisted skeins" (*Les vases communicants*, part 2); a zone of emotional turbulence has arisen in which phenomena seem to obey mechanisms of "condensation, displacement, substitution, alteration".[44] Between the sign of the event and the arrival of the event itself there is a time which can be called the time of chance. A chance occurence is what happens to time when it loses its power over the event. A chance occurrence is not the event, but it can become one (although only in a surrealist interpretation). Or, on the contrary, the event that cannot manage its own time, we call a chance occurrence.

There are ways and signs that indicate the possible presence of an 'objective chance': they are *expectancy, automatism, dreams, miracle, love*.[45] But what is, for example, a *miracle*? Intoxication, enchantment with chance, is what constitutes the miraculous. At some point, our wish is fulfilled, and chance turns into a miracle. For surrealists, an 'objective chance' is essentially no different from a miracle.[46]

The Oberiu understanding of the random is an extremely compressed history of 'that which has not happened', of that which could not have happened, but did happen only thanks to language. Language usurps the right of reality to everything that can happen. It is not miraculous or incredible, it is that which appears to have happened, but in a way that at times happens *only* in language, when even the context is meaningless. By the way, here is the difference in the interpretation of chance by Oberiu and surrealism: in the latter, chance 'throws' the poet into the real, requiring that he transform it into a miracle; the literature of Oberiu views the theory of the random as an excuse to turn to what cannot *actually* happen but that still happens in every poetic act. Then the relationship between

---

44   Ibid., 83.

45   Cf. Carrouges, *André Breton and the Basic Concepts of Surrealism*, 199ff.

46   Cf. "'Objective chance" is accessible to us only through written or oral transcriptions, narrations, or legends: Apollinaire recognised himself in the cut-out profile of a target figure in the background of a Chirico canvas. After his head wound, people tried to see in it the realisation of this sign. In 1931, Victor Brauner painted a *Self-Portrait with Enucleated Eye*; in 1938, intervening in a brawl at the painter Oscar Domiguez's, he was hit in the eye with a bottle, which knocked it out. In 1934, Breton was walking in the flea market with Alberto Giacometti and bought, moved by "elective" choice, a spoon "whose handle, when it rested on its convex part, rose from a little shoe that was part of it." He then remembered that, several months previously, he had tried to persuade Giacometti to fabricate a "Cinderella cinder-tray," or ashtray, the idea for which came to him from a fragment of a waking-phrase' (Chénieux-Gendron, *Surrealism*, 81–2).

the 'chance occurrence' and what actually happened is approximately the same as the relationship between the part and the whole, but with one addition: the part is concrete, while the whole is abstract and inaccessible (they are of different nature, so they never intersect, i.e. they do not interact). Their connection is so weak that they lose any opportunity to serve each other as orienteers in acquiring lost meaning. Thus, it is not possible to speak of, say, Kharms' 'incidence' as an occurrence or as something that *actually* happened. This is a kind of chance occurrence that cancels itself; in other words, as we have already emphasised earlier, that *falsifies* its own randomness.

A chance occurrence with a cause; everything that happened is on the surface; there is no depth, no reason for what has happened and may still happen. On the basis of such positions there opens up the ontological foundation of the Oberiu's (literary) Work as Chance (as an entanglement of the heterogeneous, the incomplete and the spatially and temporally indeterminate) – *a (literary) Work meant for nothing.*

5

Reverse Rotation

Variants

One of the most attentive researchers of play, Roger Caillois, highlights
four patterns of play activity: *agôn* (competition), *alea* (chance), *mimicry*
(simulation) and *ilinx* (vertigo). The first pair – *agôn/alea*, and the second
pair – *mimicry/ilinx* – are the best combinations. If *agôn* is a competition, a dispute, a war, a clash of interests and so on, then *alea* is a lucky
chance. Competition is primarily the will of the subject to active participation in the struggle, while *alea* requires a passive subject who relies on
a 'lucky chance', a subject who takes a risk, but who is unable to intervene
in the game itself. It is undeniable that the poet-thinker encounters the
simultaneous action of all forces of play. The poetic complex combines
competition/chance and *simulation/vertigo*.[1] The competition among

---

1   Cf. also the following: 'The vertigo first and foremost destroys his autonomy. He
is no longer a centre or a starting point, an origin of movement or a source of energy,
but a metallic shaving at the mercy of a strong magnet. He allows himself to be sucked
into the abyss. Here is an important fact: life turns out to be helpless in the face of temp-
tations that ruin it. He is pulled in by the abysses. An inopportune paralysis overcomes
him who surrenders to their enchantment. He wants to move away from the danger but
approaches it instead despite of himself. He senses that he can conceive and execute
only those gestures that would further plunge him into the abyss, as if the fatal image
of destruction, satisfying his unknown perverse preference, awakened an intimate and
merciless complicity that was a secret even to himself' (Roger Caillois, *La communion
des forts: études de sociologie contemporaine*, Marseille: Éditions du Sagittaire, 1944, 72).
In the psychophysiological scheme, this is a *rotation* around one's own axis. Fear rolls up,

poets may have independent value, but here comes a 'lucky chance': one poet overcomes another. We can assume that deep empathy can lead to poetic transformation, to a *simulation* that naturally provokes states of trance, and, first and foremost, of *vertigo* generated by sudden transitions from one state to another; however, it can also be caused artificially (with the help of narcosis or simply as a result of play). We know the feeling that we have in a high-speed elevator – its stop is expected, but we react to it with a slight sense of vertigo, because we do not notice how fast it is going. We experience a sudden disturbance of arterial pressure, an influx or sharp efflux of blood, and so on. Suddenly everything floats in front of our eyes, mixes, 'clumps together', melts, disintegrates, turns into a dredge that rises from the bottom of the well, breaking the transparent density of the water. In other words, we experience vertigo not because something is spinning in front of us or is spinning us, but because of a sudden stop; when everything floats, melts, we lose consciousness. Is the loss of consciousness the result of intense *vertigo*? Isn't that what Lipavsky is thinking about?[2] When the world slows down and begins to prepare to change its rotation in the opposite direction, we go into a trance. We lose the position that preserved the pathos of distance, that made us independent of the world, and made the world the subject of our desires. This is not only a purely physiological experience, but also a 'panic of consciousness': 'the vertigo is not a result of rotation but of fear.'[3] But where does the poetic substance come from? Is it not from this sense of fear that causes vertigo as the time of the world begins to move into a *reverse rotation*? 'Be proud that you were present at the start of the Opposite Rotation. Before your very eyes, the world was turning back into what it came from, into its primordial property-less foundation.'[4]

---

disfigures, leads toward dark and deep foundations of life, where it is already at the limit of death. No, not death, but annihilation; one confronts Nothing and emptiness.

2   Lipavsky attempted to explore this in one of his reflections entitled 'Vertigo': 'But someone can object to what was said: it is one thing when rotation, either of oneself or something in front of oneself, does actually take place, but it is another thing when this rotation is illusory, when one feels it but also understands that it does not exist. The latter case is a case of vertigo' (Lipavsky, *Issledovanie uzhasa*, 190).

3   Ibid., 38.

4   Ibid., 22. What is interesting is that Lipavsky distinguishes *movement* and *rotation*, and considers the latter as a state of consciousness, i.e. as a *false* movement: 'The movement is a change in position and distance in relation to the rest of the things. Anything can be considered either as an aggregate of elements, points (a shape), or as a whole (a point), it all depends on how we want to do it. During rotation, the whole thing (the

The individuality is blown apart, the world clumps together. It is as if the world began to turn along its axis and the poet were the first victim of this all-penetrating fear.

Thus, the first variant is *subjective*. It seems to me that it includes two types of rotation. The first type is *centripetal*: everything gathers around the ego-centre, concentrates and pulls everything else into its rhythm of rotation; there is a constant strengthening, an accumulation of the power of the 'I'. The second kind is reverse or *opposite* rotation; it is *centrifugal* rotation, which is precisely the kind that causes vertigo: sensation of falling, extension of gesture, flight, dispersion. In short, 'I' as the centre of conscious life no longer exists. This transgressive state also corresponds with sleep, drug intoxication, play and other 'liminal' experiences. These include the fundamental existentials discussed by Heidegger: terror and fear, boredom and emptiness, nothing and annihilation.

The second variant is *objective*: clockwise rotation, 'running of the clock', a universal count of world-time that accompanies the main types of 'subjective' rotation but affects them only indirectly.

Naturally, if the subject is 'thrown out of itself' by centrifugal forces, it sees the world differently, as if in a dream; the world becomes *fluid*: 'The new human thought began to move and flow. It became fluid. The old human thought says of the new one that it "went off" [went insane]'.[5] And here is another observation by Kharms: 'One person thinks logically, while many people think fluidly. I am alone but I think fluidly'.[6] Now, things and all that is visible are not correlated in accordance with their properties and subtle differences of their individual being; they *clump together*, seek to become a single material element, for example, blood and water, something jelly-like; they want to become compact, to become a lump of being, and then to achieve homogeneity and the hardness of a crystal. The *reverse* rotation leads to these transitional states of the world substance, unlike the customary rotation that is slow-willed, all-encompassing and focused on the identity of the 'I'. That is why dreams and the 'imbibing of spirituous liquors', why poetry as an element of the figurative fabric of sleep, why magical trances and all sorts

---

point) remains in the same position and at the same distance from other things as before; therefore, it is not a movement' (ibid., 105).

5   Daniil Kharms, 'Odinnadtsat' utverzhdenii Daniila Ivanovicha Kharmsa' [Eleven assertions of Daniil Ivanovich Kharms], *Logos* 4 (1993), 113.

6   Ibid.

of *transformations*, turn out to be signs that reverse rotation is gaining momentum. Perhaps rotation should be understood as a return of the world-time to slow and small perceptions, to 'decay of consciousness'. It is not the rotation of things, but of ourselves; it is the release of forces protecting the firmness and the boundaries of the 'I'. That is when the poet challenges, blows up established poetic and scientific norms, orients himself to the unique, the unexpected, introduces chance into the world and thus renews chaos. The symmetrical world is replaced with the asymmetrical world that is becoming mobile and fluid. It is the sort of deep trance that the members of Oberiu often referred to.

In dream-like mythical worlds everything is constantly renewed and yet there is nothing new. Some worlds fall apart, and new worlds are formed from the wreckage. Everything is determined by *chance* that brings order to chaos and chaos to order. Something resembling a kaleidoscope. Lévi-Strauss used the model of the kaleidoscope in relation to the logic of mythical thinking:

> This logic works rather like a kaleidoscope, an instrument which also contains bits and pieces by means of which structural patterns are realised. The fragments are products of a process of breaking up and destroying, in itself a contingent matter, but they have to be homologous in various respects, such as size, brightness of colouring, transparency. They can no longer be considered entities in their own right in relation to the manufactured objection of whose 'discourse' they have become the indefinable debris, but they must be so considered from a different point of view if they are to participate usefully in the formation of a new type of entity: one consisting of patterns in which, through the play of mirrors, reflections are equivalent to real objects, that is, in which signs assume the status of things signified.[7]

The way a collection of colourful pieces of glass, falling into the mirror reflection, creates one of the combinations of regular patterns is similar to the ordering of the 'raw material' of the myth by means available to thinking. This is an example of consciousness where chance acts not through destruction but through creation. A single turn or even half a turn of the kaleidoscope tube changes the pattern (as if in a dream). Thus, the pattern

---

7   Claude Lévi-Strauss, *The Savage Mind*, Chicago: University of Chicago Press, 1966, 36.

depends on the number of reflective mirrors, the presence of coloured glass, the speed of turning, the intensity and the regularity of rotation. But is that not what happens in any other game? Before throwing dice, we shake them to ensure success (and cards need to be shuffled); otherwise, the 'unlucky draw' may be repeated. Shake it a few times and hope for a 'lucky' outcome. In the kaleidoscope we only get a pattern when we rotate the tube, but the number of patterns is always limited. Rotation creates seeming order out of the random elements that are not connected in any way other than by being placed next to each other. A repetition of patterns may give their adjacency an appearance of similarity. This rotation says nothing about time itself, because it does not affect it. The myth repeats itself; it does not need the idea of time. Here time is frozen in the relationship of things to each other; there is no time inside the things.

A high degree of randomness in the production of patterns (the role of chance) creates conditions for poetic *nonsense*, which makes *sense* only in the design of the kaleidoscope itself. Nonsense is 'a small deviation', which, if repeated, creates a fiction of equilibrium for the entire *mythosystem*, endowing it with meaning. This is not unlike what happens in a 'house of mirrors' at an amusement park: when we enter it, we fall under the influence of mirrors placed a certain way and see ourselves in so many reflections that we lose contact with our own image; now it cannot be distinguished from all the mirror images.

Let's take a closer look at the examples of rotations that are relevant to Oberiu's poetry of 'stopped world-time'.

(1) *Direction: horror. Rotation-1.* Is fear possible as an ontological characteristic of the world's objectness? When we pass on to the object the ability to cause fear, we transpose fear into another emotional register – into fright. After all, only fright can be connected with time, understood *as a point*, atomistically, since fright is something unexpected, it is a jab, a breach in a peaceful environment of fulfilled expectations. Fright does not refer to fear as a feeling that develops our ability to evaluate reality. Often, fright is an instinctive reaction to a possible touch (it can be of any intensity and duration; it can be different in strength and force of action, in distance). In the expanded definition, fright is a consequence of sudden loss of the object, and this object is the desire itself. Lipavsky has a wonderful formula: 'In a human body the erotic is that which is scary.' Lipavsky's *The Study of Horror* is not at all about horror. The first fear that

gives birth to horror is the fear of 'standing water' that 'closes over one's head like a stone'. All these homogeneous spaces, which stopped accumulating the heterogeneous, stopped being porous, condensed, empty, firm, oscillating and so on. Since the heterogeneous is eliminated, the world-time ceases to exist.

> Fear of the dark. When someone is walking through a forest at night, this fear is understandable. But even a child knows that there is nothing to fear in a dark room. But he is afraid, nonetheless. Taking a closer look at this fear I note in it a fear of isolation or loneliness; an expectation of unknown threats; a boredom of uniform background. The latter one I understand. Didn't I talk about it when I talked about fear of high noon? Uniformity destroys time, events, individuality. It is sufficient for us to hear the sound of a siren to feel the whole world moving to the background with all our affairs, to feel a touch of non-being.[8]

Deserts of water, snow and sand; the frightening magnificence and excessive 'energy' of tropical nature – all of these are extremely dangerous if, following boredom, they give rise to a longing for action that could resist the power of nature over a particular life. And here comes insanity: 'a man with a knife runs away without stopping, he wants to cut out, to cut open the continuity of the world; he runs, killing everyone in his way, until he is killed or until a bloody foam starts pouring out of his mouth'.[9] So what? Why does water cause such increasing horror? Why does blood? Why do many other things that can stop time turn out to be able to nourish our soul and give the world its properties? We belong to the world as physical, solid bodies, and as soft, susceptible warm-blooded organisms; we possess a particularly sensitive flesh; but we are wild animals with passions, we are bodies-plants that know no time; we are bodies-liquids, bodies-atmospheres; we are bodies of fear; and, at last, we are demons, werewolves and vampires. In a word, at the intersection of many probable and mysterious environments, we form a certain individuality and give it a human name.

Another example: the position of the *eyes*. Let us imagine for a moment a different kind of eye movement, a reverse kind. It is this that Lipavsky called *the reverse rotation*. Then we have before us a sad series of ossified,

---

8   Lipavsky, *Issledovanie uzhasa*, 35.
9   Ibid., 23.

deadened, blind eyes. . . Let us remember that 'the world stands before you as a muscle seized with a spasm, as a pupil frozen from tension', and 'the ossified pupil will consume you as well'.[10] The eye turns from that which sees into that which is seen, and this seen eye has nothing to do with the eye we have come to think of as the organ of human sight. Now the light of the world is no longer the divine light, but the light without god. As Bataille (a contemporary of Kharms and Vvedensky) remarked, such an eye, popped from the eye socket, is a *dead* eye. As another poet put it:

> The whole room hung on this thin, barely real, and yet so apparent feeling, as on a softly trembling axis, and then on the two people upon whom it depended: the surrounding objects held their breath, the light on the wall froze into golden lace . . . everything was silent and waited and was there only for them; . . . time, which ran through the world like an endlessly glittering thread, seemed to move through the middle of this room, and seemed to move through the middle of these people and seemed to suddenly pause and become rigid and still and glittering . . . and the objects moved a little closer to each other. It was that stillness and then soft kind of sinking, as when surfaces suddenly arrange themselves to create a crystal . . .[11]

The members of Oberiu are probably correct: in order to see the world as it is in itself, one needs not a living eye, an active, selective, 'precise' eye supported by divine guarantees, but a 'dead eye', an eye that is completely open, with 'eyelids that cannot be closed', an eye that is neutral to both the darkness and the light of the world. A bone-eye, a tree-eye, a water-eye; an eye that can withstand the cessation of time, that is prepared to accept light from any source or dimension of time, even if this time is too slow and reminds us of our own death. An eye that has lost consciousness, turned inside the eye socket, a sleeping, dreaming eye, a crystal-eye . . . that is probably the eye of the Oberiu poet-thinker. The cessation of the world-time is a loss of energy; anywhere where the force of compression/entanglement/tightness is in effect, a different temperature regime emerges: everything cools off.

---

10   Ibid., 21.

11   Robert Musil, 'The Completion of Love', in *Unions: Two Stories*, trans. Genese Grill, New York: Contra Mundum Press, 2019, 3.

Another example: you have a dream. You are guilty of something, whether you have committed murder or some disreputable act that no one should know about; you think everything will be revealed. A sense of fear grows as you realise the 'irreversibility' of your crime, which you may not have committed, a sense of fear growing into horror. Here is where the effect of the incredible reveals itself: that which wasn't supposed to happen becomes reality that manifests itself against the background of a rising wave of fear. Out of this fear, you forget that you are sleeping and that this is all a dream. Your guilt of *this* 'crime' appears so obvious that there is no doubt: who else could have done it but you? Still, behind the distinct 'reality' of the dream lies the question: is it not absurd that I would have committed such a 'crime'? A typical situation for any dreaming person caught in the trap of a nightmare. It is absurd, but it is you, and it is the reality of your dream, and you must take it seriously. That is when we are overcome with horror, the horror of hopelessness; now only the interruption of the dream can save us from a heart attack, and the arrival of such a fear makes our blood freeze in our veins, makes our heart stop. The pure form of fear is the horror that comes to replace it, that is what nightmares are. The experience of horror initiates the waking mechanism. After all, it is the *awakening* that saves the world from the curse of 'stopped time'. The prince wakes up the sleeping princess with a kiss, brings her back into the world she left behind, but she must not lose the time itself, the time that she owns. Poetry is precisely such a dream. A deep dream that suddenly turns into a dream-like reality, then into a nightmare. And here is the moment of awakening . . . A kiss by a prince from a fairy tale is a call; to kiss is to call by a name, a call is a call out, a giving or a receiving of a name, i.e. it is not just a call (of nature or passion). What was almost lost is being restored: meaning, fate, anticipation of future death and so on. In order to learn what the world is like without us, we must stop time, we must separate it from the world and from ourselves. A dangerous enterprise. For the moment when an observer suddenly sees a star of time rising, the same happens to him as what is happening to the world: he 'grows cold', becomes 'ossified', 'fossilised', 'grows heavy and eternally calm'. Essentially, he dies . . . It is at this moment that one must find the strength to hear a call, a call of a still living but fading time that belongs to an observer who is far from being immortal. The transition into a world without time, into a timeless world, is probably like jumping (transition) into the depth of a dream: one dives in and immediately comes back up. One must remember to come back to the surface before one loses the memory of language and all that still remains of it and helps us resist death in a deep 'dead' dream, that still beats within us like a frightened heart, namely, our own name. A call out allows us to *call back*, to come back from the depth; to cross the threshold of the world's end and to come back. But who is calling us out? As strange as it sounds, it is not Soul or God, but Language!

It is this report about one's adventures in the world of stopped time that will become Oberiu's (literary) Work.

But what is happening here? The answer may seem arrogant: is it possible to imagine what happens to the world when the language ceases to function? Inside the language, in the very depths of it as a system of diverging differences, there is ancient law of calling out: 'Say your name!' The call is answered only by someone who acquires the meaning of existence through language. To call out the world by its name is to use this naming in order to permit one thing and to forbid, to draw closer or to push away another thing. This is the world that the poetics of the members of Oberiu is concerned with. We should have realised this sooner. Vvedensky and Kharms 'know' this world well, and they look at its structure through what Mamardashvili called the 'unpatched holes of being' which open up in a variety of dream-like experiments: in dream-vision, in deep meditation, in sniffing of ether, and, finally, in a poet's play with death. In the world as it is, nothing happens, it simply endures, but endures in a time that is not commensurate with the time we experience in our individual existence, where we use time to solve language problems, and refer to ourselves using 'I', challenging the flow of time that stands against our 'I'. If we assume that the reality of the world is given to us by language, and that language in turn controls the image of reality, then, naturally, once the language ceases to be the agent of control, the time of the world begins to 'slow down'. Nothing like that can happen in the *real* world. Everything that happens, happens only to us, beings of language. A new proximity to the world opens up; language no longer prevents the world from capturing us. The world falls away from the language, plunges us into chaos and the nonsense of random images; this is the natural environment of the Oberiu poet. Is the bravery of the members of Oberiu found in their lack of fear in face of chaos, i.e. in face of a *world without language*?

(2) *'Flickering of the world'. Rotation-2.* What do we mean by 'ethereal freedom'? Ether sniffing is not an innocent prank, a game, or just a desire to expand one's experiences. Of course, it is partly all of these. And perhaps the members of Oberiu used all these experiments to try to confirm their vision – who knows? When one reads Vvedensky's reflections about his dreams of death, one understands that such a hypothesis cannot be rejected outright. In what follows below I emphasise what requires a special comment:

> *More than once, I felt that I both understood or did not understand Death.*
> Here are three occurrences that I firmly recall.
>
> 1. I was sniffing ether in the bathroom. Suddenly everything changed. Where there had been a door, an exit, a fourth wall appeared from which my mother hung hanged. I recalled then that this was precisely the death foretold as my own. Never had anybody foretold my death. *A miracle is possible at the moment of death. It is possible because death is the stopping of time.*
>
> 2. In prison, I had a dream. A small yard, a field, a platoon of soldiers, someone is to be hanged, a Negro it seems. I experience a great fear, horror and despair. I ran. And as I ran down the road, I realised that I had nowhere to run. Because *time is running with me and standing still with the sentenced one. And if we imagine its area, it's like one big chair on which both of us will sit down simultaneously.* Afterward, I'll stand up and walk on, and he won't.
>
> 3. Another dream. I was walking with my father and either he told me this or I realised it myself: that today in an hour and a half they'd hang me. *I understood it, I experienced a stop. And something for real and finally come. That which has really happened is death. Everything else is not that which has happened. It's not even that which is happening. It's a belly button, the shadow of a leaf, it's a skid on the surface.*[12]

---

12   Alexander Vvedensky, *The Gray Notebook*, trans. Matvei Yankelevich, New York: Ugly Duckling Press, 2002, 10. Emphases added.

We may say that the poetic sensibility of the members of Oberiu is, at its source, *ethereal* (or dream-like); however, the ether itself does not open the way to new states of the world, but rather chemically confirms what is possible as a vision. To create from death. But death now must be perceived as a special mechanism for the transmission of what is experienced into a spatially accessible image. The mechanism of transition is the state of death. Not death, but the *state* of death. That means everything that helps one reach the state of death (*not-now*): sleep, ether, poetic inspiration and so on. That is the only way to get rid of boredom. When we talk about the *clumping* of the world, I once again simply repeat with Vvedensky and Kharms: when the world begins to clump together, it begins to flicker. What is this 'flickering'? Take a look at Castaneda's texts and you will find the same basic categories of Oberiu's experience (though devoid of dramatism and existential responsibility). You will find even the terminological overlaps: same 'point of assembly', same rhythms of 'flickering', same 'slowdown', same 'speed'. But flickers can be instants of novelty, and hours of *boredom*. *If we see flickers* in a world limited by language, then we are bored, but if we embrace the slowness of a world outside of language, where every flicker is an event, and then everything is new. Boredom is superiority of repetition over an instant of novelty; novelty is an excess of the unrepeatable in one instant. The world is flickering not only because you are high on ether, but because any attempt to go beyond the boundaries prescribed by language, if successful, reveals that flickering is our fundamental possibility of being. But of being as if before oneself, before my own 'I' and before others. But that is impossible! Yes, but the poetry of Oberiu makes it possible. The forces of clumping are correlated with the rhythms of flickering. Flickering and clumping are events of the same order. Any flickering signifies a certain *rhythm*. Here is this well-known statement by Vvedensky:

If time were a mirror image of objects. In reality, objects are feeble images of time. There are no objects. Go on, try and grab them. If we were to erase the numbers from a clock, if we were to forget its false names, maybe then time would want to show its quiet torso, to appear to us in its full glory. Let the mouse run over the stone. Count only its every step. Then each step will seem a new movement. Then, since your ability to perceive a series of movements as something whole has rightfully disappeared, that which you wrongly called a step (you had *confused* movement and time with space, you falsely *transposed* one over the other), that movement will begin to *break apart*, it will approach zero. The shimmering [flickering] will begin. The mouse will start to shimmer [flicker]. Look around you: the world is shimmering [flickering] (like a mouse).[13]

So, the world is flickering like a mouse skittering on a stone; therefore, to understand the flickering of the world, it is necessary to comprehend the run of the mouse, its every single step. What does Vvedensky teach us? He connects this comprehension with a nominal reduction: at this point we do not know what 'step' means, nor what 'every' means, nor what 'stone' means; we do not even know what 'mouse' means. At this point, we do not know any names, and all we see is a flickering of multiple 'points of time' that have split up the movement of the mouse into so many segments that the mouse turned into continuous flickering. As we look at it, we are trying to count these slipping instants of flickers, but our effort is in vain, the time stops its course, the mouse ceases to be the mouse and becomes the world. In other words, the word 'mouse' can no longer be either the signifier or the signified, and the language cannot hold the points of time in a sequence; it cannot control the inconceivable speed of the world. The smallest constituent parts of time cannot be named, they are points, instants; they can only flicker. These instants, or 'points of time', are too different from one another for us to believe that just now they belonged not to the world but were the run of the mouse.[14] The designation 'mouse' no longer exists and the language is incapable of demonstrating that this is not the case. What conclusions can be drawn from this by the thought of Oberiu? The first, and perhaps the most important one: parts, or, better, particles of the world exist as they *are*, outside of any whole (for example,

---

13   Ibid., 11–12. Emphases added. See Druskin on 'flickering': 'How do I represent the world to myself? In the form of flickering. Only in flickering, and not in many flickers but just in one instant. And this one flicker is similar to the course of thinking, not only of abstract thinking but also of thinking in space, that is, of thinking that comes into existence thanks to a new coordinate, as I already said in "Symphony" . . . Then in the second part – in "Numbers" – this one real flicker should be described as it appears – as a system. Then, as the unsecured network of knots unravels into a thread, so this system disintegrates into *nothingness*' (Druskin, *Dnevniki, 1928–1962*, 255–6).

14   A beautiful image of time: 'Points fly about the world; these are points of time. They settle on leaves, they descend on foreheads, they make bugs happy' (Vvedensky, *The Gray Notebook*, 15).

outside of 'language' or 'consciousness'). A particle of the world exists in another particle of the world, not as its part, but as an equal and independent particle; particles are immutable in their individuality (quality, signification, modality), but this individuality expresses itself in entanglement with other particles. They may, for example, form the time of the mouse, or the time of the world; they clump together but do not mix. The world is consumed by the time of the mouse, but the mouse itself cannot escape from the time of the world.[15]

Time is something attached to the world; the world itself simply *is*, it is timeless. A person is a temporal being, and it is he who introduces a temporal dimension into the world, noticing various changes and comparing them one against another.[16] The change is noticed only as a result of the substitution of the rhythm of one form of existence with another. Every self-contained being has its own rhythm, thus a hierarchy of rhythms is formed where each rhythm is different from all other rhythms. And at the top of this hierarchy, there is a *global* or *universal* rhythm.

> The world as a whole has no time, because it is an isolated system, a *single rhythm*. But this is, properly speaking, an unrepresentable world, because, in trying to represent something, we already look at it as if from the outside, so we violate its isolation.
>
> And this 'world *almost* as a whole' would already have time, its own time, different from any particular time, main time, 'river of time'. That is why, while, in abstract terms, one could select any change as a basic change (for example, one's pulse or the fall of a stone), in reality,

---

15   See another explanation of 'flickering': 'NM [Nikolai Oleinikov] considered himself a specialist of entoptic vision. He was interested by what was going on inside his eye. He observed spots or blurs, "stars" and textures. The spots float slowly at the edge of the field of vision until they disappear. The stars make continuous movements like a cloud of gnats in the evening before the arrival of good weather. The textures are large, pale and immobile. There are other textures, coarse-grained, they look like algae or sea animals . . . NM., on the basis of the differences of movements of these bodies and their sizes (he calculated them), establishes what a person sees in his eye. He also believes that the spots are quite far from the bottom of the eye, and float away when one wants to bring them to the centre of vision. Stars or bright points, by contrast, have independent movement' (Leonid Lipavsky, 'Razgovory [Conversations], *Logos* 4 (1993), 13 [7–75]).

16   Cf. 'One can imagine that a changing element, such as a grinder with his rotating wheel, has joined a stable and thus timeless world. It is curious and noteworthy that this one-and-only changing element would seem to overpower all other countless changeless elements: with its arrival, the world would acquire time counted with the help of a wheel's turn. If the wheel is stopped, the time will disappear' (Lipavsky, *Issledovanie uzhasa*, 72).

there is only one kind of change that one could select – the 'global rhythm' that we are more or less able to perceive. Muhamad's saying 'time stands still but you are moving' is correct in the sense that the global rhythm has no stages, it is not a change, it is not temporal, but it becomes such only in relation to an individual rhythm that does not coincide with it.[17]

The world as a rhythm would be extratemporal.[18]

It is the rhythm that, like aqua regia, dissolves in itself all other rhythms, and no comparative scale can be applied to it. The transition from one individual or local rhythm to another is instantaneous. This transition is a cessation of time, a certain pause that links, by dividing, two spheres of being: that which *is* and that which *becomes*. A pause is just a blink-of-an-eye, but if we experience it *from within*, then in it the time slows down, imitating eternity.[19] The global rhythm subjectively corresponds to the altered states of consciousness: dreaming, deep meditation, narcotic intoxication and ecstasy. Life consists of such transitions, switches or interruptions, of changes of rhythms; that is why poetry is larger than life: it is the rhythm of rhythms. Or, as Lipavsky put it: art is the 'summoning of rhythmic states', 'a hierarchy of rhythms', while time understood existentially is the 'discrepancy' of rhythms.[20]

(3) *The egocentricity of the inner speech. Rotation-3.* Lev Vygotsky's concept of the *inner speech* can serve as a model for understanding non-sense in Oberiu's poetry. The inner speech is *egocentric* and does not have the intentions of dialogical *external* speech; it moves within the infantile

---

17   Lipavsky, *Issledovanie uzhasa*, 111–12.

18   Ibid., 96.

19   The dream is a sort of a hieroglyph of the instantaneous transition from one rhythmic experience to another. An important note: 'Inner landscapes – temporary hieroglyphs – are special (rhythmic) states, states of art' (Lipavsky, *Issledovanie uzhasa*, 94). In other words, phantasms, daydreams, poetry and dreaming can be equated with each other, these are all instantaneous events. That which endures is eternal, that which does not endure *possesses* time. The relationship between the line (eternity) and the point (time). The eternal is a kind of change that includes all others, or it is that for which there is no scale of comparison. Time that revolves around its own axis without changing anything is Eternity.

20   Lipavsky, *Issledovanie uzhasa*, 94–6. On 'time as a discrepancy of rhythms', see ibid., 108.

flickering consciousness. Here we witness an unprecedented experience of the *appropriation* of language. Before acquiring conscious verbal skills, a child goes through the preparatory stage of the 'childish babble', a stage of constant mumbling, when the pleasure of articulating sounds is, in some way, comparable to the pleasure of eating (oral ecstatic). Therefore, the inner speech is incomprehensible by *nature* (not by *function*), because it is a residual image of the inner elaboration of certain contents that are becoming one's consciousness, contents that a child cannot yet endow with an 'exact' meaning. Such contents are idioms, omissions, 'asyntactic fusion', fluidity, continuity.[21] Here is what Vygotsky writes regarding this:

> External speech is a process that involves the transformation of thought into word, that involves the materialisation and objectivisation of thought. Inner speech involves the reverse process, a process that moves from without to within. Inner speech involves the evaporation of speech into thought. However, speech does not disappear in its internal form. Consciousness does not evaporate and dissolve into pure spirit. Inner speech is speech. It is thought that is connected with the word. However, where external speech involves the embodiment of thought in the word, in inner speech the word dies away and gives birth to thought. To a significant extent, inner speech is thinking in pure meanings, though as the poet says, 'we quickly tire of it'. Inner speech is a dynamic, unstable, fluid phenomenon that appears momentarily between the more clearly formed and stable poles of verbal thinking, that is, between word and thought.[22]

Now we understand why Vygotsky did not turn to the literary tradition of the *inner flow* of consciousness.[23] Is it possible that he regarded

---

21   See Lev Vygotsky, *The Collected Works of L.S. Vygotsky. Volume One: Problems of General Psychology*, trans. Norris Minick, New York: Plenum Press, 1987, 277, 279: 'The increasing manifestations of this tendency for an *asyntactic fusing of words* in the child's egocentric expressions parallels the drop in the coefficient of egocentric speech.' And further: 'In its internal use, each word gradually acquires different colorations, different sense nuances, that are transformed into a new word meaning as they become established. Our experiments show that word meanings are always idiomatic in inner speech, that they are always untranslatable into the language of external speech. The meaning of the word in inner speech is an individual meaning, a meaning understandable only in the plane of inner speech. It is as idiomatic as an elision or password.'

22   Ibid., 280.

23   After all, Vygotsky knew and valued the work of William James, who was the first

the child's inner speech only as a stage of development (or, more precisely, 'underdevelopment') that had no analogues in the adult psychical experience of language? In my view, he traced the reflection of internal processes of correlation of thought and word not in their fluidity and mobility, but in their static states. Essentially, we witness the intellectualisation of the activity of consciousness as that which differentiates and gives rise to meanings. Therefore, the word is a fragment of a yet unrevealed meaning, an empty sign, rather than a symbol endowed with meaning. The supremacy of meaning over significance leads to linguistic loss and destruction. In other words, we are talking about a meaning produced by a poetic imagination that transcends any linguistic expression; and the child's naive, 'unspoiled' consciousness possesses such an imagination. The poet is such a child.

---

to formulate the idea of the inner flow of consciousness. And there are plenty of examples of the 'fluidity' of the inner life of consciousness of characters in Russian literature, for example in Tolstoy, Dostoevsky or Chekov.

6

Conversations

A Community of Friends in Time

I will tell you honestly how our thought is made, where conversations come from, how words fly from one interlocutor to another. You need to sit quietly for a while, trying to catch a small star so that, as they say, you had a reason to exercise your neck for turning your head toward friendly known and unknown interlocutors.[1]

How beautiful is a disinterested conversation! Nobody wants anything from anyone, and everyone talks when they want and about whatever they want. It is like a river: it flows and moves towards the sea now slowly, now quickly, sometimes it goes straight, sometimes it turns right or left. Two goddesses stand behind the conversation partners: the goddess of freedom and the goddess of seriousness. They look at everyone kindly and with respect, and they listen to the conversation with interest.[2]

---

1   Daniil Kharms, 'Skazhu tebe po sovesti' [I will tell you honestly], in *Polnoe sobranie sochinenii* [Complete collected works], Volume 1, St Petersburg, 1997, 207–8.
2   Lipavsky, *Issledovanie uzhasa*, 26.

Interest: To Converse (in) Conversations . . .

One of the forms of Oberiu existence that pre-dates and justifies a creative
effort is *conversation*. The art of carrying on a conversation: talking-
conversing, *conversation* [*raz-govor*] is both a slander [*o-govor*] and a
spell [*za-govor*] ('don't pull the wool over my eyes!'); to converse is to cast
a spell but also to deceive. At the beginning of *Conversations*, recorded
by the philosopher Lipavsky, the interests of the members of Oberiu are
organised into separate groups:

> N.M. (Oleinikov) said: Here is what I am interested in: food, numbers,
> insects, journals, poetry, light, colours, optics, interesting reading,
> women, Pythagoras and Leibniz, pictures, structure of living spaces,
> rules of life, experiments without instruments, problems, recipes,
> scales, global conditions, signs, matches, shot glasses, forks, keys and so
> on; ink, pencil and paper, writing methods, art of conversation, inter-
> actions with other people, hypnotism, homegrown philosophy, people
> of the twentieth century, boredom, prose, cinema and photography,
> ballet, writing things down daily, nature, 'Alexandro-Grinovshchina',
> history of our time, experiments on myself, mathematical actions,
> magnets, use of various objects and animals, enlightenment, forms
> of infinity, liquidation of disgust, tolerance, pity, cleanliness and filth,
> forms of boasting, inner structure of the earth, conservatism, some
> conversations with women.

> N.A. (Zabolotsky), responding to the same question, said: architec-
> ture, rules for large structures. Symbolism, depiction of thoughts in
> the form of conditional placement of objects and their parts. Reli-
> gious practices. Poems. Different simple phenomena – scuffle, lunch,
> dancing. Meat and dough. Vodka and beer. Folk astronomy. Folk
> numbers. Sleep. Positions and figures of revolution. Northern nations.
> Destruction of the French. Music, its architecture, fugues. Structure
> of depictions of nature. Domestic animals. Beasts and insects. Birds.
> Goodness-Beauty-Truth. Figures and positions in military operations.
> Death. A book and how to create it. Letters, signs, numbers. Cymbals.
> Ships.

D.Kh. (Kharms) talked about what he was interested in. Here is what he was interested in: writing of poems and learning different things from poems. Prose. Enlightenment, inspiration, illumination, super-consciousness, and everything related to it; ways to achieve it; finding one's own system of achievement. Different kinds of knowledge not yet known to science. Null and zero. Numbers, especially those not connected into a sequence. Signs. Letters. Fonts and types of handwriting. Everything that is logically meaningless and ridiculous. Everything that is funny, humorous. Silliness. Natural thinkers. Old omens and new ones invented by someone. A miracle. Magic trick (without props). Human, private relationships. Good tone. Human faces. Smells. Destruction of disgust. Washing, swimming, bath. Cleanliness and filth. Food. Preparation of some dishes. Presentation of the dinner table. Structure of a house, an apartment and a room. Clothes, for men and for women. Issues related to wearing clothes. Smoking (pipes and cigars). What people do when they are alone. Sleep. Notebooks. Writing on paper with ink or pencil. Paper, ink, pencil. Recording events daily. Recording of weather. Phases of the moon. The way sky and water look. The wheel. Sticks, canes, wands. Anthill. Small short-haired dogs. Kabbalah. Pythagoras. (My own) theatre. Singing. Church service and singing. Ascots. Women, but only of my type. Sexual physiology of women. Silence.

L.L. (Lipavsky) is interested in: Time. Transformation and annihilation of space. Non-existence and non-material existence (e.g. smell, warmth, weather). Study of death. How an individual case is possible. Global lines, words, hieroglyphs. Body, height, breathing, pulse. Sleep and dreaming about yourself. Shining, transparency, fog. Wave. A shape of a tree. Origin, dissipation and change of sensations. Gamma, spectrum. Colour black. Meaning of feelings (e.g. horror, vertigo). Lack of persuasiveness of mathematical proofs. Structure of a circle. Rotation, angle, straight line. Chess board as its own world. Paradise, morality and duty. Rules of life. Happiness and its connection to certain substances and consistencies. Cleanliness. Meaning of beauty. Outskirts, empty lots, fences; poverty; prostitution. Inventories, encyclopaedias, dictionaries, hierarchies. Ancestors, Jews. Types of women. Causes of sexual attraction. Fates of lives. A trajectory of revolution. Old age, reduced needs. Water, current. Pipes, galleries, small tubes.

Tropical feeling. Connection of consciousness with space and identity. What a tram conductor thinks about during work. Hair, sand, rain, sound of a siren, membrane, train stations, fountains. Coincidences in life. Sense of duration during social events when one has already lost all sense of interest, irritation, boredom and fatigue. Same facial expression of different women at certain points in time.[3]

Here is the cause of 'conversing (in) conversations' – the *interesting*. It is interesting to talk about something, interesting to interact socially, interesting to argue, interesting to be next to someone, interesting to do something together. Interest is spontaneous, unpretentious and purely random, it moves constantly, it transcends the limits of an individual person and attaches itself to objects that the person seeks to acquire – this is how these objects become interesting. Interest is a temporal category, at times destructive to an individual if he cannot keep it strictly aligned with the intended plans and goals; therefore, each I is in question as soon as the interest is weakened or lost.[4] On the contrary, for a collective or a group entity, the marker of 'collectivity' is not *interest*, but *play*.[5] One can be interested in something *only individually*, but one can only play a game with someone, i.e. together or collectively. There are play-related peculiarities here. For the experience of Oberiu, perhaps the circle of readers is quite narrow, or, if we put it more dramatically, they simply have no readers (in the traditional sense). The space of the game is locked in its orientation on the Other who is immanent to the relations that are constructed in the game. One can say that there is the space of the game, or the 'place' where it occurs; and this is not just a specific physical space of a common room or an apartment, a hall, a prison cell, a place of

---

3   Lipavsky, *Issledovanie uzhasa*, 307–10.

4   Cf. 'At the root of both vice and inspiration lies one and the same thing. At their root lies genuine interest. Genuine interest is the most important thing in our lives. A man with no interest in anything will quickly perish. An overly one-sided and powerful interest increases the stress on life exponentially: just one more little push and a man goes out of his mind. A man cannot fulfil his duty if he lacks true interest in it. If a man's true interest coincides with his duty, he will become great' (Kharms, '*I Am a Phenomenon Quite Out of the Ordinary*', 486).

5   Of course, there is a 'game of interest', and the game itself (practically, any game) is a clearly shown interest in precisely this form of occupation. But this is too general, as we are talking about interest in a more Kierkegaardian sense: *inter-ecce*, to exist *between*, or, more precisely, to exist not in *a place*, but between *places*, to exist in motion, or, to be more precise, in a jump, in a transition.

their dreams and hallucinations. There are also players who are capable of surprising one another; this is the defining thing in these endless examples of mockery, pranks, ironic putdowns, challenges and simulations. The genuine Other is someone who already played the role of a reflected image of the questioning 'I'. This 'one's own', sometimes unrecognisable Other is what is common for all the members of Oberiu.

Conversations is a book about a multitude of interests, recorded without reviewing what was listed, and is almost reminiscent of automatic writing. In the conversations, there seems to be present something unconscious, which each participant is not so much exchanging with others as presenting as evidence of his poetic gift. This is what inner time intersected by the fragments of poetic events might have looked like. *Conversations* is a collection of different pieces of information and 'knowledge', discretions and tricks; it is not a conversation of one person with another, and not an attempt to understand, to 'interpret' the meaning of the Other's utterances: 'It is interesting that they did not listen to one another, but, as a result, they were quite satisfied with each other.'[6] *Conversations* is where each member of Oberiu talks about his own interests, but in a way that does not prevent others from doing the same. Every participant in the conversation thinks and talks from a point in the present, from a temporal givenness, from 'now-time', and does not cling to the past. Personal interest is not found in one particular realm, but is diverse in terms of selected objects, and we cannot limit their number.[7] The four Oberiu collections of what they find to be interesting cited above form intersecting sets with no boundaries. In the course of the conversations, the exchange of interests takes place constantly; the conversation continues when one is alone with oneself as a kind of friendly echo of speeches of others that runs ahead of everything personal. It is true that an individual always individualises his own interest. To the extent that the interest is directed at something specific, the individual aims to turn it into a permanent and strong attraction, to preserve his engagement with the subject matter of interest. Here is the paradox of a collective subject: an individual, consisting of a set of interests, will not grasp the objects of interest until he is

---

6   Lipavsky, *Issledovanie uzhasa*, 319.

7   Kharms' 'Diary' has an entry about what he is interested in and what he loves. This list only partially overlaps with the list provided by Lipavsky. See Kharms, 'What Interests Me' and 'What I Love' in *'I Am a Phenomenon Quite Out of the Ordinary'*, 378–80.

involved with them individually. But access to them is difficult: they are scattered and immersed in the exterior time; they are part of the global collection that is not yet assembled into one whole, they belong to the collective.

What is the difference between conversations and, for example, social interaction, communication, dialogue or the old genre of having a conversation with oneself? A dialogue is not just a conversation, unrestricting and random, popping up here or there; it has a specific purpose: *mutual understanding*. To enter into a dialogue means, therefore, to overcome hostility and rivalry, to find ways to understand the position of the Other. The Oberiu conversations did not restrict their participants in any way. One person talks, then another person talks, then a third person talks; they each talk about their own things, there is no development, no one overarching idea. How are these conversations organised and what are they built on? On the same common experience of the time of the present. But what if we suggest that 'conversations' have a different principle than, for example, a principle of *inter-action* or *dialogue*? Maybe it is more about inter-participation in a common thought and life? This is the space of a perfect friendship (where everyday aspects of behaviour can overlap with the high and elevated aspects, and, in turn, be treated ironically, played with, directly mocked or bullied, without leaving the realm of amicable participation). In speech, there is competition and challenge; the stronger the response to an enemy attack, the more such speech depends on the reaction of others. To speak, but in order that the Other can hear. And this is a permanent feature that guides the conversations of the members of Oberiu.

The Other is the closest person to oneself, perhaps closer than Buber's 'Thou'.[8] Gadamer underlines the *hermeneutic* status of the *conversation*, presuming that all those who are conversing are equally participating in the search for meaning (or in the process of 'discovering' it). For him, conversation is productive when it is deployed in a clear environment of the understanding of the language in which the two participants communicate. Conversation between two participants is always an attempt to translate what stands between them and without which understanding is impossible as such: 'language is the universal medium in which

---

8   Cf. Martin Buber, *I and Thou*, trans. Ronald Gregor Smith, New York: Charles Scribner's Sons, 1958.

understanding occurs'.[9] In fact, Gadamer avoids talking about *misunderstanding*, presuming that the real purpose of conversation is to understand one another. The members of Oberiu consistently demonstrate the opposite point: the foundation of conversation is *mis-understanding*; only misunderstanding draws one into the process of conversing where it demonstrates the untranslatability of what is said into what is understood, where it defends the autonomy and integrity of the former. A misunderstanding is an insurmountable boundary that the members of Oberiu storm in their conversations, but which they can nonetheless never cross.[10] The unity in misunderstanding is the unity of interests – interests in one another.

Kharms' self-portrait
(mid-1930s)

Theatre for Oneself: Pseudonyms, Ciphers, Apartments of Daniil Kharms

At times, it is easier to 'understand' the members of Oberiu not as being in a dramatic conflict with their time, but rather as independent of their time; to see them (despite their violent deaths) not so much as jokers or city lunatics, but as playing a serious role; to acknowledge their right to choose their own mask and manner of living – *living-in-defamiliarisation* from real experience by translating it into poetic experience, thus erasing all traces of any contact with the threatening reality of the political regime of their time. Many researchers are inclined to give more weight precisely to this notion of 'play': performance, jokes, 'pranks', provocations and so

---

9   Hans-Georg Gadamer, *Truth and Method*, trans. Joel Weinsheimer and Donald G. Marshall, New York: Continuum, 2004, 390.

10   Cf. 'In conversations, one moves from one topic to another as if by some law; then suddenly, one leaves one line of conversation and starts another. I would like to learn the laws of conversation. To do this, to establish them, I will have to investigate much more broadly, as a mathematician, who, when dealing with a particular task, seeks the most general formula that includes cases that do not actually occur. I want to create a mathematics of conversation' (Lipavsky, *Issledovanie uzhasa*, 414).

on. After all, Kharms' attempts to encrypt some of his diary entries are related to a certain ritual of impersonation, an obvious act of *playing-at-something*. At first glance, Kharms' ciphers are determined by a presence of erotic phantasm; he encrypts entries that are in one way or another connected to sexual desires.[11] One may, of course, regard the encryption of one's own experiences as a way of hiding them from oneself, even of freeing oneself from them. In psychoanalysis, such an operation is called *repression*. It is true, however, that the repressed is not what is encrypted, but what is hiding behind it. Successful psychotherapy consists precisely in the ability to remove all symptoms, to make them inaccessible for repeated negative emotions. On the other hand, encryption is an instinctive reaction to the 'gaze of the other', to prying and surveillance, although in an era of total terror this kind of self-defence is no less dangerous. Many commentators-decipherers were somewhat disappointed by the 'non-coincidence' of the deciphered content and the efforts necessary for the development of the cipher itself. The mystical Egyptian-priestly side of Kharms' work, as well as that of other members of Oberiu, appeared to be part of their own game. The game/play stood above everything else, which meant that autopoiesis or the poetic remained a permanent dominant of Oberiu's creative imagination.[12]

Kharms' pseudonyms are part of Oberiu's theatre. Pseudonyms open the way to understanding the complex attitude of the author, his 'I', toward himself; they are a kind of auto-biographical reflection. What does it mean to use a *pseudonym*, and how, for example, is it different

---

11 Cf. 'The qualification of absurdity [*zaum'*] as a method of encryption of anti-Soviet propaganda may be related to the witness statements by Igor Terentiev, arrested in Dnipropetrovsk on 24 January 1931. According to these statements, the "lack of subject matter" that was shared by all these groups, from Malevich, Mansurov, Filonov, Matyushin and their students to Oberiu led by Vvedensky and Kharms, was, on the one hand, a method of encrypted transmission of information about the Soviet Union abroad . . . and, on the other hand, the same "lack of subject matter" was an ideological and technical foundation for counter-revolutionary work of all sorts of formalism' (Mikhail Meilakh's introduction to *Poety gruppy Oberiu* [The poets of the group 'Oberiu'], St Petersburg, 1994, 16). The authorities of the time felt acutely both this challenge to the regime and this escape from it, and pursued any attempt by artists to detach themselves from the regime, to retreat into depths, into a spiritual crypt. The escapism of Terentiev, Vvedensky . . . The hopelessness was there already in the very poetic gift of the members of Oberiu, in that each of them was totally alien to the recently created mass of the Soviet people: the nonsensical nature of the Oberiu language already condemned them. In other words, their poetic speech itself was a political cipher.

12 Alexandrov, *Risunki Kharmsa*, 238, 244.

from a mask? Pseudonym and mask make sense in the context of a game with the Other. If Kharms addresses himself, it means he knows something about himself that he can change in the eyes of others, or he thinks that such change is possible. To be an actor for oneself.[13] But this is only one side; the other side is more complex. A doubling, a *defamiliarisation* vis-à-vis oneself, expresses itself in one's choice of designation. To be the Other, not to be Oneself – that is one of the conditions for the emergence of a new name, a name that is not the name of the Father. This is the challenge that Andrei Bely throws at his father; it is the refusal of the father's name in Stendhal (Marie-Henri Beyle) and Sergei Eisenstein. One can point to something similar in the practice of pseudonyms in Kierkegaard and Nietzsche. This is especially true of Stendhal, who, in part due to the habit of a professional diplomat, in part for other reasons, encrypted not only important government documents, but also personal diaries, notes and statements, at times in the most comical manner.[14] Stendhal created pseudonyms in order to brag, in order to demonstrate aristocratic manners, in order to appear attractive to himself. But most importantly, he resolved the relationship between his own self and the Other in favour of 'I am for myself'. The Other is given a pseudonym, not a name. To put it more clearly: one should avoid names; the name does not exist at all. 'I am for myself' is a point of escape from the Other, and from the one who is already establishing a connection with the side of 'I' that is open to society. Jean Starobinski is correct to describe Stendhal's principle of *egotism* precisely in terms of a constant escape from himself and the Other.[15] It could be said that this relationship with oneself as with the

---

13   A 'theatricalisation of oneself' as Kharms' main method of life was described well by Anatoly Alexandrov: 'During his short life, Kharms created a detailed system of behaviour that included everything from his clothing and his own alphabet to his poetic incantations and masks-pseudonyms. The meaning of the system was to help the artist resist the inflexibility of everyday life and to live with a romantic determination for higher values. Or, in the words of Kharms, to be ready for a "flight to heaven"' (Anatoly Alexandrov, 'Chudodei. Lichnost' i tvorchestvo Daniila Kharmsa' [The miracle worker. Person and work of Daniil Kharms], in Daniil Kharms, *Polet v nebesa* [A flight to heaven], Moscow, 1991, 15).

14   Cf. an important observation: 'And the pleasure of codes is at the same time to divide language, and to speak *twice*' (Gérard Genette, *Figures of Literary Discourse*, trans. Alan Sheridan, New York: Columbia University Press, 1982, 152).

15   According to Starobinski, Stendhal has a clear tendency to transformation – an exciting game of donning a new body and a mask. Literature is a great means for this: 'Stendhal dreams of occupying several bodies at once. The metamorphosis he desires is not a depersonalisation but a multiplication of the self, indeed a "super-personalisation."

Other models the relationship with society. Unlike for Kierkegaard and even for Bely, for Stendhal, pseudonyms are, on the one hand, a purely literary game, but, on the other, a sharp disassociation from everything that he cannot possess. In any case, the wisest of his critics pointed this out.[16]

> For a long time now, I have loved dreaming up apartments and their furnishings. Sometimes I would draw up a mansion with eighty rooms, but at other times, I like an apartment with two rooms.[17]

> To sit in your room and to know that you are completely taken care of and to draw up apartments.[18]

> The apartment and everything connected with it is an entire world: disintegration, destruction, exposure – bodies, feelings, worlds. God help us.[19]

In Kharms' diaries we find drawings of apartments: especially in 1928, 1930, 1934. In Kharms' design experiments, it is not the drawing itself that matters, but the filling of the apartment space: furniture of various purposes, beds, ottomans, nightstands, bathrooms, tables, kitchen and living room accessories, chairs, sofas and so on. An ideal private space, a place for meeting and living with friends. The obsessive repetitiveness of Kharms' 'apartment' drawings is a testament to his ideas regarding a space that is concealed and comfortable enough to accommodate the creative work of his entire group of friends. In this case, escape into the inner

---

He wants to become not just *an* other but *several* others' (Jean Starobinski, 'Pseudonymous Stendhal', in *The Living Eye*, trans. Arthur Goldhammer, Cambridge, MA: Harvard University Press, 1989, 89).

16   For example, Paul Valéry wrote: 'As for egotism à la Stendhal, it implies a faith, the faith in a *natural Self*; and education, manners, and *morals* are its enemies.' And in another passage: 'Literary Egotism consists, in the last analysis, of playing the part of one's *self*' (Paul Valéry, *Collected Works of Paul Valéry, Volume 9: Masters and Friends*, trans. Martin Turnell, Princeton: Princeton University Press, 1968, 188, 191). In essence, Valéry is trying to separate the natural and the conventional Ego, and to make the natural retreat under the onslaught of the conventional.

17   Daniil Kharms, *Zapisnye knizhki. Dnevnik: Kniga 2* [Notebooks. Diary: Book 2], St Petersburg, 2002, 209.

18   Ibid., 195.

19   Druskin, *Dnevniki, 1928–1962*, 539. This entry was made in 1942, during the blockade of St Petersburg, on a windowsill next to Kharms' apartment that had been nailed shut.

space acquires a special meaning; Kharms' apartments are his enduring symbol.

The idea of a crypt, a hidden place, an escape from reality into a hidden realm of private interests, influenced the entire philosophical-metaphysical, and broader poetic, practice of Oberiu. The apartments are an adventure and an escape into an unreachable life that is not simply desirable (it is impossible). Kharms uses his drawings of 'apartments' the same way he uses the encryption of texts. The meticulousness of the drawing of a particular apartment space is surprising; it contains the possible number of occupants, the size and number of rooms, the location in the urban environment, but the most important part is the allocation of space for meetings-conversations with friends.[20] Encryption requires certain operations; the same are required for marking up the interior space of apartments: both should be filled in, and each time anew and with different things, with a new set of rooms of different sizes. So, what do we see? As in the case of deciphering, in the first place we see *combinatorics*: moving, shifting, overturning, expanding and so on. These sketches of apartment drawings show Kharms' desire for an anti-communal and sufficiently comfortable private space (something from the pre-revolutionary times). As with the encryption entries, the 'apartments' are part of the diary combinatorics full of numbers, letters, dictionaries and alphabets.[21]

---

20   Cf. Kharms, *Zapisnye knizhki. Dnevnik: Kniga 2*, 21: 'Me and my wife – 1. My office, 2. The library, 3. A small living area, 4. Bedroom, 5. My wife's room, 6. The dining room, 7. The living room, 8. An extra room; Dad – 1. The office, 2. The bedroom; Natash – one room; Mashenka – one room; Common spaces – 1. Large hall, 2. The dining room, 3. An extra room, 4. An extra room; Liza and Volodya – 1. The office, 2. The bedroom, 3. The dining room, 4. Child's room, 5. A small living area, 6. A room for au pair. 8+2+1+1+4+6=24.' This is how, according to Kharms, his new apartment's rooms would be assigned and occupied.

21   In another diary entry Kharms writes: 'To create a "machine of philosophical ideas"' (Daniil Kharms, *Zapisnye knizhki. Dnevnik: Kniga 1* [Notebooks. Diary: Book 1], St Petersburg, 2002, 406). And such machines are special, they produce the random and the unexpected, they prepare us for a miracle, in fact, for a cessation of time. See also the following: 'The power of words must be liberated. There are such combinations of words in which the action of power is more noticeable. We should not think that this power will make things move. Although I am sure that the power of words can do that as well. But the most valuable action of this power is almost indeterminable. The rough example of this power is seen in the rhythms of metric poems. The complex ways that metric poems help a body move should not be treated as something made-up. These are the crudest but also the weakest expressions of the power of words. The further expressions of this power

The Land of Messengers

> If a person can become a co-author of someone else's thing, then he
> does not need to know the history of philosophy. Vvedensky, Lipavsky,
> Kharms, Oleinikov were indeed the co-authors of 'Messengers', that is
> why Kharms could say: 'I am a messenger.'[22]

Oberiu as a poetic group has three forms of linking up into a collective
author: *touching* (members of Oberiu) – *invading* ('Chinari') – *absorbing*
('messengers'). I pass by, tangentially, *touching*, but do not get involved,
and immediately leave without returning (the return can take place only
along a long arc). A light interaction is not a dialogue, but, at the very
least, it is listening to the Other, taking its position into account. But here
I *invade*: I move to meet the Other actively, often aggressively, provoking a
backlash, but the advantage remains with me. I invade the territory of the
Other with my own idea, I take a risk, but if there is a reciprocal interest,
the collective author acknowledges my contribution, and even leaves me
with the right to the idea I expressed. Finally, there is *absorption*: my idea,
my method or my thought are absorbed by the Other; this is more than
just an appropriation, it is saturation and the subsequent development
of someone else's thought as one's own. Someone else's thought ceases to
belong to its originator and now belongs to the collective author, i.e. every
member of the group. Hence the closeness of common destiny, word,
place and time, habits, inclinations; their differences, although noticeable,
are not significant from this point of view, nor do they define them as
poets. In other words, how they differ does not eliminate their depend-
ence on one another, which they need to be the Other for themselves and
for everyone else. Here is a fragment of their earlier manifesto:

> each of us has his own creative face, and this is confusing to some. They
> talk about a *random* combination of *different* people. Apparently, they

---

are hardly available to our rational understanding. If one were to think of the method for
studying these powers, then this method must be completely different from the methods
used so far in science. A fact or an experience cannot serve as proof in this case. I can't
tell what can be used to prove and verify what was said. So far, I know four kinds of
word-machines: poems, prayers, songs and incantations. These machines are built not
by calculation or by reasoning, but by another way called "alphabet"' (Kharms, *Zapisnye
knizhki. Dnevnik: Kniga 2*, 174).

22   Druskin, *Dnevniki, 1963–1979*, 296.

think that a literary group is a kind of monastery, where all monks look the same. Our association is free and voluntary, it connects masters, not apprentices – artists, not house painters. Everyone knows who he is, and everyone knows how he is connected with others.[23]

Later, Druskin quite rightly believed that the group's work should, despite all the differences, be considered as a single act of creation by one Author (precisely with a capital letter). That is what we should think about, instead of trying to discover in this group the separate and isolated individualities of its authors. Kharms was a genius, that much is true, but all the others were geniuses as well: Vvedensky, Lipavsky, Oleinikov and others. Druskin does not engage with the spiritual heritage of his fallen friends randomly; he does not attempt to appropriate their convictions, or dissolve them in his own reflections, in the mysticism and metaphysics of post-Oberiu time.[24] What happened was quite different: he was trying, but now by himself, to continue to communicate with them, to remember them, to once again raise those questions that seemed to have gone away with them forever. . . The members of Oberiu entered our time through Druskin, and they did so with the force of presence that *only* living characters of thought and poetry can possess.[25] Druskin's division of the group is extremely curious: at first, there is a purely external creative organisation of poets, formed to present a manifesto, and this group consists of the *members of Oberiu*; then, a little later in time, we see the emergence

---

23 Anatoly Alexandrov, ed. *Vanna Arkhimeda* [Archimedes' bath], Leningrad, 1991, 458.

24 At first glance, Druskin's position seems peculiar: he was the one who not only survived all of his friends – and that was indeed a privilege of fate – but also the one who saved the archives of Vvedensky and Kharms (what was left of them). True, in the last decades of his life, he increasingly assumed the role of a religious metaphysician, believing himself to be responsible for the *correct* understanding the work of Oberiu. At times, when reading Druskin's reflections, one might get the impression that the members of Oberiu had no choice but to go through poetry to the true faith. However, the problem of discussing the choice of path of tragically departed poets *post mortem* is not eliminated. In Druskin's reflections, God exists in different forms, not only *faith-based* but also *figurative, conceptual*, even purely *instrumental* forms. For Druskin, God is a universal substance within the boundaries of which the private metaphysics of faith is deployed, or what he himself called *metatheology*. Perhaps, though with a certain caution, one should speak of the secular nature of Druskin's faith, a faith outside of the church.

25 Cf. 'In the end, the death of D.I. (Kharms) was an indispensable sacrifice. To make it less meaningless and horrible, I have to start writing again' (Druskin, *Dnevniki, 1928–1962*, 133).

of 'Chinari' as a group of close collaborators and friends.[26] True, Druskin was not satisfied with his own explanation of the group's authorial unity. In his diaries, he often talked about the opposition between the notion of personal immortality and the violent death of his friends. Later, inspired by a new idea, he tried to present the group's unity in terms of an ancient, four-part division of human temperaments, on the basis of the union of natural elements. Here is what he came up with:

> If the four natural elements are taken without any additional value, simply as four properties of life, or rather, four kinds of ability to have a property, equal and similarly necessary for life, then Kharms would primarily be represented by *earth*, Lipavsky by *water*, Vvedensky by *air*, and myself by *fire*.
>
> Lipavsky – *Tractate on Water*; in 'theory of words' there is a first projection of the seed of the word onto a liquid; his interest in Thales and the element of water. Bach has the same motif of water as bliss. Schweitzer did not notice this. In Lipavsky, water is a symbol of the impersonal elemental life, the immersion into which is both scary and blissful.
>
> Kharms – not-quite-humans, *The Old Woman*. And what about the miracle? In the sense in which it is realised in Kharms, it is also connected with earth: a miracle in 'Incidences'. The element of earth is in no way lower than other elements: 'mother-earth'.
>
> Vvedensky. The air is everywhere and covers everything: earth, water and fire. An almost classical completeness and perfection of his works, clarity and transparency in texts like *Sutki* [Twenty-four hours] or *Potets*. Vvedensky's lightness is also air.
>
> The earth is opposed to the sky, or the air as a symbol of the sky. What is common between the two is that both are all-encompassing: the sea and the ocean are not bottomless, the bottom is the earth, same

---

26 Cf. 'Here is something that many of the researchers of Kharms' work do not understand: his personality was not determined by his extravagance in clothing or by his public conversations with people he did not know or could be open with, or by the memories of him of those very same people (although not all the memories of Kharms are like that), but by his interactions with friends, their creative mutual influence, which can only be assessed by a comparative analysis of the works of all 'chinari'. There is still a misconception about Kharms and his work, based on Kharms' two-year participation in Oberiu (The Union of Real Art), an exoteric society of poets united only for external purposes' (Druskin, *Dnevniki, 1963–1979*, 508).

with the water on earth; the air covers everything: earth, water and fire. Earth and air are juxtaposed as materiality and immateriality, as heaviness and lightness. Water is juxtaposed with fire: we say, 'as incompatible as fire and water'.[27]

This is what this relationship would look like:

air
being-less-ness
(Vvedensky)

water
less being-less-ness
(Lipavsky)

fire
less being-less-ness
(Druskin)

earth
being-ness
(Kharms)

Community as a movement of natural elements; it differs depending on the element; water moves horizontally, fire vertically: from the earth up to the sky, into air which makes souls and deities fly. Carl Jung and Gaston Bachelard's theories experimented with similar poetic experiences. Thus, for Bachelard, the peculiarity of poetic experience depends fully on natural elements, their power, strength or weakness. A unified author is located at the centre of poetic imagination, and imagination in its deep substantial forms is connected with the living matter of four basic elements. Bachelard's thought (and it gives us the best opportunity to understand poetry, even a 'meaningless' kind) is that imagination is the exit of sensuous experience beyond its own limits. In order for the image to be present, to be visible, it must be saturated with the matter of the chosen element, with its properties that can be expressed in language with sufficient completeness. Every poet is supported by a native element of poetic imagination; it is deeply individual and unique, like a pattern,

---

27   Ibid., 420. Kharms tested similar distinctions on his own experiences: 'We propose dividing all works of art into two camps, Fire and Water. Let us explain by way of examples: 1) If you walk through the Hermitage you get a Watery feeling from the galleries housing works by Cranach and Holbein and from the galleries where gilt silver and wooden church sculptures are exhibited. 2) From the Spanish gallery you get a Fiery feeling, even though here too you will see examples of purely Watery phenomenon [sic] (monks with ribbons coming out of their mouths)' (Kharms, 'I Am a Phenomenon Quite Out of the Ordinary', 474–5).

a particular frequency, a quivering of properties of water, fire, earth or air: 'an image is a plant which needs earth and sky, substance and form'.[28]

In the 1930s, Druskin actively discussed with Kharms and Oleinikov the emergence of a new poetic being that symbolised the spiritual individuality of the group's members: the being's name was the *messenger*. This was what could provide the whole group with a sacral identity, pointing out the 'kinship of souls' and images. The messenger not only brings the news, it is also an 'angel' – a special being who lives at the intersection of two worlds: it looks into our world, but from its own *other* world where it resides permanently. The messenger is a soul that is already in another world but also here with us, in our world. Being a messenger is a fragment of the *angelology* of poetic experience. If early *Oberiu* was first and foremost a political or a formal association of poets for a purely external purpose, then '*Chinari*' was a phenomenon of creative friendship, a 'close-knit circle' of friends.[29] So then the *messenger* was something purely ideal, the non-human or super-human in a human being, not a function, but a soul, an 'angelic rank'.[30] Let us attentively reread Druskin's text 'Messengers and Their Conversations' (1933):

> What are messengers talking about? Are there events in their lives? How do they spend the day?
>
> The lives of messengers pass in immobility. They have the beginning of events or the beginning of a single event, but then nothing happens, the origin belongs to time.
>
> Time is between two instants. It is emptiness and absence, the lost end of the first instant and the anticipation of the second. The second instant is unknown.

---

28   Gaston Bachelard, *Water and Dreams: An Essay on the Imagination of Matter*, trans. Edith R. Farrell, Bloomington: Indiana University Press, 1983, 3.

29   Cf. 'Oberiu could be considered an *exoteric* organisation – an association of poets who presented their work together; but *Chinari* was an esoteric association that also included Leonid Lipavsky and Nikolai Oleinikov' (Alexander Vvedensky, *Proizvedeniya* [Works], Volume 2, Moscow, 1993, 164).

30   Of course, one must remember here the legendary mythology that the founders of the rather narrow literary community, Oberiu, invented for domestic consumption. The more connections with the outside world weakened and grew increasingly hostile, the more important were the signs of poetic and human chosenness. The messenger is the legendary character of the poetic play, he must save the poet from a future horror that has crept very close to him.

An instant is the beginning of an event, but I do not know the end of it. No one knows the end of the events, but messengers are not afraid of this. They do not have the end of events, because *there are no intervals between instants.*

Is their life monotonous? Monotony, emptiness, boredom – all these come from time. They happen between two instants; and between two instants there is nothing to do.

Messengers cannot connect two instants together. But they observe the original connection of the existing and the non-existing.

Messengers know the order of other worlds and various ways of existing.

When I cross a railroad at a certain point, I put my foot between the rails, trying not to touch them. Messengers do this better than me. Besides, they know all the omens and therefore live in peace.

Messengers have no memory. Although they recognise all the omens, they discover them anew every day. They discover every omen with an occasion. And they also know nothing about what does not affect them.

Messengers talk about forms and states of surfaces, they are interested in the smooth, the rough and the slippery; they compare the curvature and the degree of deflection, they know numbers.

A tree is attached to its location. In a particular place, the roots come out of the ground in the form of a smooth tree trunk. But the distribution of trees in the garden or in the forest does not obey any order. So, the place where roots come out and become a trunk is random.

Trees have an advantage over people. In their life, the end of events is not lost. For them, the instants are not connected. They know no boredom or monotony.

Messengers live like trees. They have no laws and no order. They have understood *randomness.* Another advantage of trees and messengers is that for them nothing is repeated, for them there are no periods.

Is there an advantage in having a possibility for free movement? No, it is a sign of a disadvantage. I think those who have the possibility of free movement lose the end of an instant. Free movement creates periods and repetition, as well as monotony and boredom. Immobility based on random location – that is what does not repeat. If this is the case, the messengers are attached to a particular place.

How long do messengers live for? They do not know time, and

nothing happens for them; their lives are not calculated in our years and days, our time, but perhaps they have their own measure of time?

Perhaps they have their own instant and the end of that instant is lost, just like ours? Maybe they talk about emptiness and absence? Their emptiness is scarier than ours.

Messengers know the opposite direction. They know what's behind things.

Messengers observe. How buds open up on trees. They know the location of trees in the forest. They counted the number of turns.

Messengers know the language of stones. They achieved an equilibrium with a small deviation. They talk about this and about that.[31]

And here is a later version, from Druskin's diary (1943):

O. (Oleinikov) imagined messengers in the form of bottles with colourful fluid displayed in the window of an apothecary. Indeed, messengers are immobile and attached to a place, but they freely penetrate bodies, space, the plane of nature, and they can be imagined in the form of a vessel filled with reason, emotion and, undoubtedly, sensation. Sensation is a particular sort of understanding. In the hierarchy of immaterial beings, messengers are higher than me. Below me are demons and devils. They are semi-human, although they lack bodies. They should not be compared with animals. Animals, on the plane of nature, have their own mind and in some way are smarter than devils, while devils are semi-intelligent beings, and their weakness of mind is not substituted by any natural mind. In scholastic terminology, they lack substance or essence – *ens*. Both animals and humans, and perhaps even plants, are beings; messengers are super-beings, and devils lack being, they are incorporeal semi-humans.

Let us say more about corporeality. I mean natural corporeality, but there is another kind of corporeality that is found, perhaps, in a certain sort of concentration, in a thickening of the mind, in attention, in intensity of feelings, intensity of sensations. At that time, both messengers and demons have bodies. But for us, these are changing bodies: they disappear, then suddenly appear, they change. Precisely

---

31   Yakov Druskin, 'Vestniki i ikh razgovory' [Messengers and their conversations], *Logos* 4 (1993), 91–2.

because messengers are immaterial, they are attached to a place: plants and trees move, even a stone changes its place over time, but the messenger, having found himself in a place at an intersection of his plane and the plane of nature, will remain there. While being everywhere, it is as if he is in one place. The plane of nature, life, and death. The state of life and sensations – all these are 'I' who is escaping me.[32]

The elements of Druskin's reflections may be put together to reconstruct a general portrait of these extraordinary beings – messengers: *beings that do not exist . . .* Or, to put it differently, their non-existence is existence, but not for us. They are attached to one place, but this place itself is not a place for visible, sensed existence, therefore this place is present *everywhere*. The negation ('non') overcomes existence with non-existence. Messengers exist on their own, for their existence does not depend on our existence. That is why they are so mysterious and are absent everywhere; they are like trees because nothing can interrupt their growth and development. For them, there is nothing random; in them, the random acquired the property of constant change; they have the most direct link to natural events and matters, for example, water. Let us recall that water is the main element of Lipavsky. The chosen element endows the messenger with its poetic properties, and, as we know, there are four elements. What do we see? We see the fiery messengers of Druskin; the grounded, faithful to Earth and existence messengers of Kharms; and finally the floating and airy messengers of Vvedensky.

It is unlikely that Kharms would have agreed with this description. This is what he writes down at the precise moment of the messengers' arrival:

Something banged in the clock and then the messengers came to me. I didn't realise right away that the messengers had come to me. At first, I thought that the clock was broken. But here I saw how the clock kept running and was, in all likelihood, showing the correct time. Then I decided that there was a draft in the room. And then I wondered: what kind of phenomenon is it that a clock running wrong and a draft in the room can equally serve as cause? As I thought this over, I was sitting on the chair near the couch and looking at the clock. The minute hand

---

32 Druskin, *Dnevniki, 1928–1962*, 168.

was on the nine and the hour hand near the four: consequently it was a quarter to four. Beneath the clock there was a tear-off calendar, and the pages of the calendar were rustling as if a strong wind were blowing in the room. My heart was pounding and I was afraid of losing consciousness.

– I have to drink some water, – I said. On the end table next to me there was a pitcher of water. I stretched out my arm and took the pitcher.

– Water may help, – I said and started looking at the water.

But here I realised that the messengers had come to me, but I could not distinguish them from the water. I was afraid to drink the water, because by mistake I might drink up the messengers. What does that mean? It means nothing. You can only drink a liquid. But really, are the messengers a liquid? That means I can drink the water and there's nothing here to fear. But I can't find the water. I went around the room looking for it. I tried shoving a strap into my mouth, but it was not water. I shoved the calendar into my mouth – it wasn't water either. I said the hell with the water and started looking for the messengers. But how could I find them? What do they look like? I remembered that I couldn't distinguish them from the water which means they look like water. But what does water look like? I stood there thinking. I don't know how long I stood there thinking, but suddenly I trembled.

– Here's the water! – I said to myself.

But it wasn't the water, it was simply that my ear had begun to itch.

I started to root around under the dresser and under the bed, thinking at the very least to find there the water or a messenger. But all I found under the dresser in the dust was a ball that had been chewed through by a dog, and under the bed some shards of glass.

Under the chair I found a half-eaten cutlet. I ate it and I felt better. By now the wind had nearly stopped blowing, while the clock ticked calmly showing the correct time: a quarter to four.

– Well, that means the messengers have already left, – I said to myself and began changing my clothes to go on a visit.[33]

---

33   Kharms, *'I Am a Phenomenon Quite Out of the Ordinary'*, 489–90. A note from 22 August 1937.

When messengers come, the time of a miracle arrives. Kharms looks at the clock: a quarter to four. And, according to the hero, the clock continues to run, and it shows 'the correct time', yet a miracle is embedded in its course: the presence of messengers. Time stops for those who experience their presence and does not stop for the time itself that continues to run as usual. True, after the messengers leave, the hero notes that the time, although it was passing, turned out not to have been passing at all since the clock showed the same time: *a quarter to four*. One can only assume that the hero's 'experience', and therefore the presence of the messenger, took place in the time of a miracle, the time that cannot be measured and does not run like the time of the clock. The messenger-poet is the true subject of time that stops. . .

At first glance, a comparison of a messenger with a plant is surprising. Why or what for does Druskin use this risky comparison? I think he does so in order to develop the idea of a miracle (Chance) for a unified poetic ontology of the members of Oberiu. Like a plant, the messenger is always in one place, he is immobile, he finds himself between the two closest instants. In other words, messengers are only viable during the time of a miracle. The time of a miracle is their realm. For them, there are no separate instants, their time cannot be enumerated, measured or subdivided.

Messengers, like plants, have no nervous system, they do not move in space, they do not need a purpose or a plan, they are in a kind of time that, to us, appears completely random and even impossible (such as the time of an angel or a saint). 'Messengers live like trees. They have no laws and no order. They have grasped *randomness*. Another advantage of trees and messengers is that for them nothing is repeated, for them there are no periods.'[34] Indeed, messengers as plants do not need to connect instants together, creating for themselves what was (the past) and what will be (the future), because for them there are no gaps in existence; there is but one *impulse* that they follow, something along the lines of Bergson's *élan vital*. The messenger does not have a body, the body only appears on occasion when it is necessary and then it immediately disappears; messengers have 'changeable bodies', which arise from 'one thickening of the mind'. Thus, since there is no body, there are also no senses (no neural fibres); since there is no movement, messengers are something devoid of the essential,

34   Druskin, 'Vestniki i ikh razgovory', 91.

the essence, *ens*; they are super-beings. For the poet, messengers are evidence and indicators of ways to save oneself from time that is about to stop. Indeed, the messengers' world, which a true poet enters, lies beyond the boundaries of current and perceived time; it is not even parallel to ours; it is different: it has one language, one set of feelings for many things and experiences. Messengers, like poets, create without looking at themselves. They lack a centralising instance of the Ego; they are not required to establish a reciprocal connection. Moreover, they do not have the sense of space that we have, because, remaining in place, they are always in the time of a miracle that makes each place equal to any other place, and therefore, being in one place, they are in all places.

During the time of Socrates, such beings were considered to be 'geniuses of the human race', guides to other worlds, explorers, and, of course, messengers; during other times, they were feared as though they were demons. By an effort of his imagination, the poet acquires a second nature, a messenger's nature, and creates forms. Where do the messengers hide? Where they will never be found – between instants, where time is equal to itself, where time is interrupted by nothing, by no randomness, where time does not exist at all. However, any movement by a messenger could create interferences in the course of human time; therefore, they move together with their own world, and they are only changed by their realm (plane or duration) of origin. Messengers can be understood as observers of meaninglessness, they are the souls of poets; their non-existence is in what they think and recreate; they are, indeed, messengers, because they bring messages about the wealth of other, non-existing worlds. There are no messengers as such, we are all messengers of some non-existence, messengers of a world that can never be touched. And no matter how much we try to influence this world, expecting a miracle, it remains undisclosed for us. Of course, being a messenger is a beautiful game, without which it is difficult for us to imagine the members of Oberiu playing their game . . .

❧

One day, Danya [Daniil Kharms] was especially nervous.

It was Saturday. At ten or eleven in the morning we heard a doorbell
ring. We shuddered because we knew it was GPU, and we knew
that something terrible was about to happen.

And Danya told me:

– I know that they came for me . . .

I said:

– Oh God! Why did you decide that?

He said:

– I just know.

We were in this little room like we were in a prison cell, we could not
do anything.

I went to open the door.

There were three small, weird-looking characters standing outside.

They were looking for him.

I think I said something like:

– He went out to get bread.

They said:

– Okay. We'll wait for him.

I went back to the room and told him:

– I don't know what to do . . .

We looked out the window. There was a car downstairs. And we had
no doubt that they came for him.

I had to open the door. They immediately rudely, very rudely, burst in
and grabbed him. And they started taking him away.

I said:

– Take me, me! Take me, too.

They said:

– Okay, let her come as well.

He was shaking. It was absolutely horrific.

Under the convoy, we went down the stairs.

They shoved him in the car. Then they pushed me in.

We were both shaking. It was a nightmare.

We've reached the Big House. They stopped the car not in front of the
entrance, but a short distance away from it, so that people wouldn't
see him being led. And we had to walk a few more steps. They held
Danya very firmly, but at the same time they pretended he was
walking on his own.

We entered some reception room. Here two of them took him away,
    and I was left alone.
We had just enough time to look at one another.
I never saw him again.[35]

---

35   Vladimir Glozer, Marina Durnovo, *Moi muzh Daniil Kharms* [My husband
Daniel Kharms] Moscow, 2005, 107–8.